CONTENTS

Gorseinon College
Learning Resource Centre

Belgrave Road : Gorseinon : Swansea : SA4 6RD   Tel: (01792) 890731
This book is **YOUR RESPONSIBILITY** and is due for return/renewal
on or before the last date shown.

RETURN OR RENEW - DON'T PAY FINES

MA (Queensland,) PhD (London)

Longman

York Press

Acknowledgements

The author wishes to thank Margaret Atwood for permission to quote from *The Handmaid's Tale* and from manuscript materials; also Maureen Boyd, formerly of Langley Grammar school, Berkshire, and Sue Harding from Sir John Deane's College, Cheshire, for their generous assistance based on years of experience teaching sixth-form English, in the preparation of these Notes. Thanks also to the author's daughter Miranda for all her expert help in preparing this typescript.

YORK PRESS
322 Old Brompton Road, London SW5 9JH

PEARSON EDUCATION LIMITED
Edinburgh Gate, Harlow,
Essex CM20 2JE, United Kingdom
Associated companies, branches and representatives throughout the world

First published 1998
This new and fully revised edition first published 2003
Second impression 2004

10 9 8 7 6 5 4 3 2

ISBN 0-582-78436-0

Designed by Michelle Cannatella
Typeset by Pantek Arts Ltd, Maidstone, Kent
Produced by Pearson Education Asia Limited, Hong Kong

PART ONE

INTRODUCTION

HOW TO STUDY A NOVEL

Studying on your own requires self-discipline and a carefully thought-out work plan in order to be effective.

- You will need to read the novel more than once. Start by reading it quickly for pleasure, then read it slowly and thoroughly.

- On your second reading make detailed notes on the plot, characters and themes of the novel. Further readings will generate new ideas and help you to memorise the details of the story.

- Some of the characters will develop as the plot unfolds. How do your responses towards them change during the course of the novel?

- Think about how the novel is narrated. From whose point of view are events described?

- A novel may or may not present events chronologically: the time-scheme may be a key to its structure and organisation.

- What part do the settings play in the novel?

- Are words, images or incidents repeated so as to give the work a pattern? Do such patterns help you to understand the novel's themes?

- Identify what styles of language are used in the novel.

- What is the effect of the novel's ending? Is the action completed and closed, or left incomplete and open?

- Does the novel present a moral and just world?

- Cite exact sources for all quotations, whether from the text itself or from critical commentaries. Wherever possible find your own examples from the novel to back up your opinions.

- Always express your ideas in your own words.

This York Note offers an introduction to *The Handmaid's Tale* and cannot substitute for close reading of the text and the study of secondary sources.

> **CONTEXT**
>
> Something similar to the novel existed in ancient times but literary historians date the start of the novel as we know it to the early eighteenth century.

READING *THE HANDMAID'S TALE*

The Handmaid's Tale is Margaret Atwood's most popular novel, which is perhaps surprising given its bleak futuristic scenario. Atwood's contemporary fable of prophecy and warning stages a scenario of catastrophe in the near future, from which the human race is shown to be saved in a second futuristic scenario several hundred years later in the 'Historical Notes' (p. 311). The story is told like a diary or a letter, in the first person, as an eye-witness account by a young woman called Offred, who is one of the Handmaids in the new American fundamentalist republic of Gilead. It is her story of resistance and oppression and her fight for survival up to the point where she is taken away and possibly rescued from this oppressive regime. Of course the Handmaid herself has not survived, and indeed we never know the length of her lifespan because her tale is left incomplete. However, her voice and her story relayed through the edited transcript of her cassette tapes remain as testimony to the survival of the human spirit. On a first reading we are plunged into a rather fragmented narrative, and a nightmarish world where we know very little about what is going on or what is going to happen to Offred, so that we begin in a state of shock and bewilderment and proceed in a state of suspense. Only at the end do we get a wider perspective on Offred's fragmented narrative with the 'Historical Notes', though by that point we may have come to believe that the Notes offer a very distorted interpretation of the tale we have just finished reading. This disorientation effect is deliberate, for Atwood is challenging her readers to think not only about Offred's situation but about how Gilead could happen and the ways in which that society is both similar to and different from our own.

The Handmaid's Tale belongs, like George Orwell's *Nineteen Eighty-Four*, to the **genre** of anti-utopian (or **dystopian**) speculative fiction. It is Margaret Atwood's version of 'What if?' in the most powerful democracy in the world. She describes her anti-utopian project precisely in an unpublished essay 'The Handmaid's Tale – Before and After':

> It's set in the near future, in a United States which is in the hands of a power-hungry elite who have used their own brand of 'Bible-based' religion as an excuse for the suppression of the majority of the population. It's about what happens at the

CHECK THE BOOK

George Orwell's *Nineteen Eighty-Four* (1949) is a terrifying novel about a future totalitarian society where there is no privacy and where unorthodox ideas are punishable by death.

intersection of several trends, all of which are with us today: the rise of right-wing fundamentalism as a political force, the decline of the Caucasian birth rate in North America and northern Europe, the rise in infertility and birth-defect rates, due, some say, to increased chemical pollutant and radiation levels, as well as to sexually transmitted diseases.

(This material is in the Atwood manuscripts held in the Fisher Rare Book Room at the University of Toronto.)

As Atwood has said repeatedly in the novel and outside it, there is nothing here which has not been done already by somebody, somewhere. However it is as a social critique of the 1980s and a political fable for our time that *The Handmaid's Tale* is uncannily accurate. When she began thinking about the book in 1981, she kept a clippings file of items from newspapers and magazines which contributed directly to her writing. These show Atwood's wide-ranging historical and humanitarian interests, where pamphlets from Friends of the Earth and Greenpeace sit beside Amnesty International reports of atrocities in Latin America, Iran and the Philippines, together with cuttings on surrogate mothers, forms of institutional control of human reproduction from Nazi Germany to Ceausescu's Romania, plus a warning given by a Canadian feminist sociologist on threats to women from new reproductive technologies.

If you were to keep a similar clippings file now as an update of Atwood's concerns, how many of them would have disappeared and how many would still be relevant? These will include issues relating to feminism and an anti-feminist backlash, the ethics relating to methods of reproduction like test tube babies, surrogacy or cloning, abortion, pornography and violence against women, environmental issues, militant nationalism, racism, extreme right-wing political movements and religious fanaticism. The impact of 11 September 2001, with the bombing of the Twin Towers in New York and the consequent ongoing war against terrorism has raised new levels of anxiety in a globalised context. Gilead becomes more, not less, frightening because it presents a mirror image of what is happening in the world around us, only slightly distorted to invent a nightmare future.

CONTEXT

These atrocities are both historical and contemporary, and many show an obsession with controlling sexuality, especially female bodies and reproduction. As Atwood has often remarked: 'They suppress most men, but all women, and so it is in Gilead.'

On a second or third reading of the novel it is possible to identify its four major themes:

● Feminism

● Politics

● Religion

● Environmental issues

Atwood brings these themes together by choosing to write in the genre of dystopian science fiction told by a woman. Atwood is combining genres here through her use of a woman's **fictive autobiography**, writing science fiction in the feminine. What does 'writing as a woman' mean? Is there a single feminine or feminist point of view? And what difference does gender make to the writing of autobiography or dystopian fiction? These are some of the questions which will be discussed under **Critical approaches.**

 **CHECK THE BOOK**

Lee Briscoe Thompson in *Scarlet Letters,* p. 62, points out the dangers in Gilead's and any other totalitarian theocracy where 'the theocracy (situating authority in God)' becomes 'mere window dressing for the totalitarians (situating authority in themselves)'.

This is the story of a nightmarish United States of America at the end of the twentieth century when democratic institutions have been violently overthrown and replaced by the new republic of Gilead. This invented world is at once familiar and unfamiliar, and is presented with such attention to documentary detail that it has the appeal of realistic fiction. The narrator's urgent intention is to convince us that this is the way things are for her as a woman in Gilead. Yet we find at the end that she is already dead by the time we read her story and that Gilead has disappeared into ancient history. We never find out what happened to Offred after she escaped from the Commander's house, and so we are left with a sense of incompleteness. Moreover, the novel ends on a question, which we are invited to answer in our interpretation of the text.

As an open-ended novel it encourages a variety of possible readings, though this raises the question of how free we are to make our own interpretations. Of course, there is no single interpretation, though there are guidelines suggested by the text and warnings against misreadings. After all, we have a terrifying example of misreading in the novel itself, in Gilead's interpretation of the Old Testament. We would all probably agree that this interpretation is fatally flawed when we see it in practice. Then there is the interpretation of Offred's story offered by Professor Pieixoto in the 'Historical Notes'. His is a scholarly editor's reading of an ancient document (transcribed from old cassette tapes) and we may well feel that he leaves out the crucial element of the Handmaid's tale: the personality and private resistance campaign of Offred herself. The novel demonstrates that wrong or inadequate interpretations of texts are possible.

What guidance, then, is there for readers from within the novel? For a start, the prefatory material gives us some clues by pointing to the Puritan and Old Testament elements, the social **satire**, and the themes of ecology and human survival which will be so important in the tale. The 'Historical Notes' insist that Offred's story and Gilead's story are both finished. Then the final question opens up the debate again, inviting us to be participants in the interpretative process.

Critical approaches will focus on the three main topics, though different approaches will emphasise certain features, so opening up a variety of ways in which the text might be interpreted. We shall first consider what type of novel it is, using a generic approach (see **Themes,** on **Utopias and dystopias**). The most popular critical approach is a feminist one, which focuses attention on issues of gender raised by Offred's situation within Gilead and her kind of narrative. Indeed there is a plurality of possible emphases here (see **Themes,** on **Feminism**). A third approach, via **narratology**, pays attention to the storytelling method with its first-person narrator, its fragmentation and its time shifts. You will notice that the novel presents two visions of the future, for Gilead is followed by the 'Historical Notes' 200 years later. What is the purpose of this final section? (see **Narrative techniques,** on '**Historical Notes**'). A further critical approach is through close analysis of its language (see **Extended commentaries**). Atwood is a poet as well as a novelist and she is fascinated by the uses and abuses of language as a powerful instrument for resistance on the one hand and for oppression on the other.

It is worth looking closely at language in order to see the ways in which Offred manages to relieve the bleakness of her narrative.

CONTEXT

Atwood argues that it is no accident that her novel is set in Massachusetts, home of the Salem Witch Trials and site of Harvard University. The wall where corpses of those executed hang is a key location recalling both the wall round Harvard Yard and the Berlin Wall which was still in place when Atwood began writing her novel in 1984.

CHECK THE BOOK

Atwood remarked in 1982: 'I believe that fiction writing is the guardian of the moral and ethical sense of the community...Fiction is one of the few forms left through which we may examine our society not in its particular but in its typical aspects; through which we can see ourselves.' See Margaret Atwood, *Second Words*, p. 346.

Consider her use of images of flowers and gardens or of the human body, all of which suggest a different way of relating to the world from the repressive official discourse of Gilead. How does Gilead use biblical allusions? Like any **propaganda** when it is examined closely, its Bible-based **rhetoric** represents a distortion of its sources (mainly the Book of Genesis) in the interests of an official policy or ideological position. It might be seen as an abuse of the Bible rather than an endorsement of its teachings (see **Language and imagery**).

All the preceding elements need to be considered when interpreting *The Handmaid's Tale*. We are quite specifically reminded of this by the author's injunction at the beginning of the 'Historical Notes', which is coded into the name of the place where the academic conference is being held: 'Denay, Nunavit' (Deny none of it). Offred's narrative, though set in the future, is urgent and compelling in its immediacy; it also has international and historical resonances which stretch back to the Old Testament and forward into our own contemporary world.

PART TWO

THE TEXT

NOTE ON THE TEXT

The Handmaid's Tale *was first published in hardback in 1985 in Canada by McClelland and Stewart, Toronto. The following year it was published in hardback in Britain and the United States by Jonathan Cape, London, and Houghton Mifflin, Boston. Published in paperback in Britain by Virago Press Ltd, London, in 1987, it has been regularly reprinted. The edition used in the preparation of these Notes is the currently available Vintage paperback (1996), the pagination of which is identical with former Virago editions. There are several other paperback editions published in Canada and the United States.*

SYNOPSIS

This anti-utopian fable about the future is one woman's story of her life as a Handmaid in the Republic of Gilead. As a Handmaid in the Old Testament sense, whose body is at the service of the patriarchs, Offred the narrator has been deprived of her own name and legal rights. Assigned to a particular Commander for reproductive purposes, she is a virtual prisoner in his household, under constant surveillance from his Wife and the female servants. She is also forbidden to read and write or to form any close personal friendships. Her only outings are daily shopping expeditions with another Handmaid and compulsory attendance at public events such as Prayvaganzas, Birth Days and Salvagings. Once a month, she has to undergo the grotesque impregnation Ceremony with the Commander in the presence of his Wife. She continually lives in fear of being sent to the Colonies as an Unwoman if she does not conceive a child.

Trapped in such a circumscribed existence, what kind of freedom could a woman possibly have? Offred chooses the freedom of refusal: she refuses to believe in Gileadean doctrines, she refuses to forget her past life, and crucially she refuses to be silenced.

CONTEXT

The fundamentalist republic of 'Gilead' is named after a place in the OldTestament, a mountainous region east of the Jordan. (In Hebrew the name means 'heap of stones', though the region also abounded in spices and aromatic herbs.) Gilead is closely connected with the history of the patriarch Jacob, and the prophet Jeremiah was a Gileadite. As a frontier land and a citadel, 'Gilead' projects the ideal image for an embattled state, run on fundamentalist religious and patriarchal principles. See the Bible, Genesis 31:21, 37:25.

Reading the novel induces a kind of double vision, for Offred is always facing both ways as she tells her story, shifting constantly between the present and the past. We learn about the Commander and their 'out of hours' relationship where they play Scrabble and she is allowed to read, and we learn about her illicit love affair with Nick, the Commander's chauffeur. It is through that relationship that Offred expresses her hopes for a future life beyond Gilead. Looking backward, Offred tells us about her lost husband Luke and their daughter and about her mother and her college friend Moira.

CHECK THE BOOK

For Atwood's discussion of this novel, see http://www. randomhouse.com

In the face of tyranny and persecution in public life, Offred manages to tell a witty dissident tale of private lives and personal relationships, which also includes the secret stories of other women. There is the story of Moira, the rebel who manages to escape the power of the Aunts and who later reappears working at Jezebel's, the high-class brothel for army officers and foreign businessmen; there is the story fragment of Offred's nameless predecessor at the Commander's house who leaves a hidden message on the wall and then hangs herself from the light fitting. There are also stories about the Commander's Wife who used to be a television personality on a gospel show, as well as bits of gossip from the female servants and the other Wives. Offred creates a mosaic of alternative female worlds which deny patriarchal myths of women's submissiveness and silence. If women are marginal to the masculine world of public power struggles, men are shown to exist only on the periphery of this 'women's culture'. There are soldiers and guardians, there are the dead bodies of male dissidents hanging on the Wall, and there are occasional more intimate nighttime encounters, but this is a story focused on women's bodies and their domestic lives.

At the end, Offred makes her exit from the Commander's house in the black van kept to cart dissidents away. Her escape seems to have been arranged by Nick and the underground resistance movement, but Offred does not know whether she will manage to escape over the border to Canada or whether she will be taken to prison. Her voice stops when she climbs up into the truck, so we never hear the end of her story, just as she never hears the end of Moira's or her mother's or Luke's story. This novel is full of Missing Persons.

There is an epilogue to Offred's story in the 'Historical Notes'. This is presented as the transcription of an academic paper delivered at a Symposium on Gileadean Studies in the year 2195. Atwood adopts a 'fast forward' technique here, leaping 200 years ahead into a future beyond Gilead. By that time, of course, Offred is dead and Gilead itself has fallen. The paper fills in a lot of background information about Gilead and how Offred's story came to be discovered, but it also challenges us as readers on questions of interpretation. After the audience has applauded the paper there comes the signal for opening up discussion: 'Are there any questions?' The novel ends not as academic speculation on the past but as a challenge to its readers in the present.

PREFATORY MATERIAL

- This consists of a dedication to two persons – see the reverse of the title pages, and quotations from the Bible, Jonathan Swift's *A Modest Proposal* and a Sufi proverb.

COMMENTARY

The prefatory material suggests some possible approaches to the tale. Who were the two dedicatees? And what is the significance of the three quotations which form the **epigraph**?

CHECK THE BOOK
Atwood tells Mary Webster's story in her essay on 'Witches' in *Second Words* (1972).

Mary Webster was one of Atwood's Puritan ancestors. She was hanged as a witch in Connecticut in 1683, but survived the hanging and was allowed to go free. Like Offred, she was a woman who successfully flouted the law of the Puritan state.

Professor Perry Miller was Atwood's Director of American Studies at Harvard. He pioneered the academic study of American Literature and his two books, *The New England Mind: The Seventeenth Century* (1939) and *The New England Mind: From Colony to Province* (1953), have made his reputation as an authority on Puritan history.

While these two names hint at the Puritan background used for Gilead, the three quotations give us other useful information.

The first quotation, from Genesis 30:1–3, is the Old Testament story about surrogate mothers on which the novel is based. It provides the biblical precedent for sexual practices in Gilead and raises the issue of religious fundamentalism right at the beginning. It also opens the way to a feminist critique of patriarchy where women are regarded as nothing but sexual and domestic commodities.

The second quotation is from Jonathan Swift's *A Modest Proposal* (1729), a desperate plea for improving conditions in Ireland in the 1720s in the form of a ferocious pamphlet recommending cannibalism and the treatment of women and children as cattle. In using it, Atwood signals, at the very opening of the book, her thematic and **satiric** intentions.

The third quotation, taken from a Sufi proverb suggests that, in the natural world, the human instinct for survival can be trusted. It is a comment on the polluted world of Gilead where the balance of nature has been destroyed, and is also an implied criticism of the state's over-regulation of human social and sexual activities. Only things that are desirable to do have to be forbidden.

SECTION I NIGHT

CHAPTER 1

- There is an old gymnasium that appears to be like a women's prison.
- The narrator whispers in the dark, in a dormitory patrolled by Aunts and guarded by Angels.

The narrator is one of a group of young women who are being held in a makeshift prison camp in what was once a college gymnasium, controlled by two women gaolers **ironically** named Aunts, with a heavy guard outside. The narrator nostalgically recalls the games and the dances that used to be held here between the 1960s and 1980s. It sounds very like an American campus, which indeed it

---

CONTEXT

This dislocated opening emphasises the confusion and fear which characterise any totalitarian state – in this instance, Gilead.

GLOSSARY

14 **electric cattle prods** electrified pointed instruments used to control cattle, but also used by the police in US civil rights and race riots of the late 1960s. Here the term makes explicit the association between these women and breeding animals

14 **Angels** soldiers of Gilead's army, who fight in battalions with names like 'Angels of the Apocalypse' and 'Angels of Light' (p. 92). They wear black uniforms. The name is possibly also linked with the New York 'guardian angels', a paramilitary force used to curb social violence

turns out to be. This is, or was, Harvard University, which has undergone a striking transformation in this **dystopian** novel.

COMMENTARY

'Night' recurs as a section heading seven times. It always signals 'time out', when Offred's life is not under glaring public scrutiny and when she can thus escape into her private world of memory and desire.

This is a woman's **fictive autobiography**, but we do not know who the narrator is, where she is, or why she is there.

This short introductory chapter suggests that the location may be the United States of America. It manages to evoke not only regimental discipline with the lines of army cots and the Aunts on patrol but also the young women's ability to find ways of resisting the system of control. When the Aunts are not looking, they reach out to touch each other's hands and whisper their names in the dark. The chapter ends with a list of those first names secretly exchanged as they try to establish their individual identities and of course this raises the question, which one is the narrator's? During the story all but one name is assigned to someone. Could the narrator's name be the missing one, 'June'? In this first-person narrative the narrator is not addressed by any name until Chapter 24. She is then called by her Gileadean name 'Offred', so for clarity this name will be used throughout the chapter summaries.

SECTION II SHOPPING

CHAPTER 2

- The location shifts to a Victorian house, a single room.
- Offred describes her red costume and her marginal position in the Commander's household.
- She gets ready to go shopping.

> **CONTEXT**
>
> In Gilead Handmaids' real names are erased and they are known by the name of the Commander to whom they are assigned: hence 'Offred' when her Commander's name is 'Fred'. Behind this patronymic hovers Offred's real name, which remains one of the mysteries in this novel.

> **CONTEXT**
>
> The 'return to traditional values' (p. 17) signals the New Christian Right agenda on which this society is based.

19 **Martha** female domestic servant in Gilead, from the biblical story of Martha and Mary; see Luke 10:38–42. In this society, it will be noted that almost all the characters are designated by their roles, for example, Commander, Wife, Aunt, Handmaid

21 **Sororize** a reference to sisterhood, suggesting the importance of women's relationships

CHECK THE BOOK

Commenting on Gilead's dress codes, Priscilla Ollier-Morin notes the biblical prescription in Corinthians 11:6: 'But if it be a shame for a woman to be shorn or shaven, let her be covered,' and compares it with Aunt Lydia's rule for the Handmaids: 'Hair must be long and covered…Saint Paul said, it's either that or a close shave' (p. 72). See M. Dvorak, *Lire Margaret Atwood*, p. 38.

The narrator Offred describes the daily domestic routines of the Handmaids, and begins to piece together her present situation, building up her account through short scenes and fragments of memory.

COMMENTARY

There is a narrative shift of location here, and Offred sits alone thinking in a single bedroom in an old-fashioned house, where she is virtually kept a prisoner. Her image of the 'eye that has been taken out' (p.17) suggests blankness, blindness and torture. Her actions seem to follow a prescribed pattern and her old-fashioned red dress and white headgear signal her membership of a group. But who is she and what is she doing 'for the general good', this 'Sister, dipped in blood' (p.19)? As she goes downstairs to the kitchen Offred describes the layout of the house, which belongs to a mysterious Commander and his Wife, and there are female servants (Marthas) though Offred is obviously isolated from them and excluded from kitchen gossip. Her role seems to be connected with producing babies for the state.

Other enigmas are introduced here, like the sinister Colonies on the borders of Gilead for dissidents or Unwomen and Offred's reference to a man named Luke whom she remembers with obvious affection. Having been assigned to do the household shopping, Offred receives tokens instead of money from the housekeeper and sets out.

CHAPTER 3

- Offred arrives at the Commander's house as his Handmaid and meets his Wife.
- Offred realises who the Wife used to be.

The narrative begins to fill in missing details with a **flashback** to Offred's first meeting with the Commander's Wife when she arrived at the house under the charge of a policeman called a Guardian of the Faith five weeks earlier. As she walks by herself through the luxuriant garden and hoping not to meet the Wife now, Offred remembers the hostile reception when she had been delivered at her new 'posting'. There is a strong contrast drawn between the two women, one young and dressed in red, and the other elderly and dressed in pale blue. The older woman is powerful and antagonistic, and the younger one is constantly reminded of her subservient position and of the dangers threatening her if she does not obey the rules. We do not yet know what the rules are There is a strange revelation at the end, for Offred remembers that this Wife was formerly a child television personality on a gospel music show and was called Serena Joy.

COMMENTARY

Offred realises that Serena Joy, like herself, is trapped in a patriarchal system which rigidly controls all women. The rigid colour coding of the women's clothes indicates that in this society their individual identities are lost in prescribed roles.

This chapter reveals without explicitly stating it that Offred's role in the household is to be a surrogate mother, a Handmaid, bearing a child for the Commander and his ageing Wife. This is clearly not a voluntary agreement but the result of a Gileadean government order. For Offred it will be a crucial time, for if she does not produce a child she will be sent to the Colonies.

CHAPTER 4

- Offred meets Nick and Ofglen.
- The two women pass the checkpoint and Offred makes her first small gesture of defiance.
- This is the first time the word 'Handmaid' is used in the book.

Offred continues on her way, past the chauffeur Nick, who is polishing the Commander's expensive black car, to the meeting with Ofglen, her shopping companion, who is dressed in an identical red costume. Their names **symbolise** their status as slaves to masters whose names they bear. The two women have to produce passes to go through the checkpoint out to the public way. Looking at the sex-starved young soldiers at the barrier, Offred reflects that Gilead

CONTEXT

The many religious references give biblical authority to the practices in any fundamentalist society, and particularly Gilead. 'Whirlwind' (p.27) comes from Jeremiah 23:19; 'Behemoth' (p.27) from Job 40:15; 'Eye' (p. 28) from Proverbs 15:3; 'Blessed be the fruit' (p. 29) from Luke 1:42.

GLOSSARY

28 **They also serve:** Last line of John Milton's sonnet 'On His Blindness' (c. 1654)

31 **Salvagings** Gileadean public executions (see Section XIV)

31 **Prayvaganzas** Gileadean mass-religious ceremonies. Women's Prayvaganzas are for group weddings; men's Prayvaganzas celebrate military victories (see Chapter 34)

31 **Birthmobile** red minibus used to take Handmaids to witness babies' births (see Section VIII)

is deeply misogynistic, working through law to censor and if possible prohibit sexual urges in men as well as in women. She makes the point that such repression actually encourages a widespread obsession with sex, and she gives her first small gesture of defiance by teasing the guards, flaunting her forbidden sexuality as she walks away down the road.

COMMENTARY

This chapter switches back into the present.

Nick clearly does not toe the Party line, and when he winks at Offred, she senses that here is somebody who is as dissident as herself. By contrast, Ofglen seems totally devoid of personality, but on reflection, Offred decides that this may be out of fear rather than conviction, for the Handmaids are meant to spy on each other.

We realise that this is a city under siege or at war. Their bizarre walk to the shops presents the odd mixture of familiar and unfamiliar which characterises Gileadean society, where ordinary domesticity and military regimentation exist side by side, just as the biblical car brand names combine religious fundamentalism with late twentieth-century technology

CHAPTER 5

- Offred and Offglen go shopping in Gilead.
- Offred suffers from double vision.
- There are two significant encounters.

As the Handmaids walk to the shops we learn this is a former university town, now the capital of Gilead. Offred recognises it all because she lived here before with Luke, her former husband. We share Offred's condition of double vision where the present shops with their biblical names like 'Lilies of the Field' (p. 35) and 'All Flesh' (p. 37) and the queues for rationed goods and the Econowives all insistently remind her of how life used to be so different in 'the time before' when she was a free woman. She remembers Luke and their young child, and in her loneliness she yearns for them and her

CHECK THE BOOK

See George Orwell's *Nineteen Eighty-Four* (1949) where similar abuse of language to that perpetrated in Gilead as a means to hide the truth is a feature of the totalitarian regime.

CONTEXT

There are more biblical references: 'Gilead is within you' (p. 33) alludes to the Bible, Luke 17:21, 'the kingdom of God is within you', of which Aunt Lydia's statement is a variant; 'Lilies of the Field' comes from the Bible, Luke 12:27; 'Milk and Honey' (p. 35) reminds us of the Bible, Exodus 3:8 and 17, where the Land of Canaan is described as 'a land flowing with milk and honey'; 'All Flesh' alludes to 'For all flesh is as grass, see the Bible, 1 Peter 1:24.

old friend Moira. There are two significant encounters here: one where the pregnant Handmaid Ofwarren (formerly Janine, whom Offred recognises from the Rachel and Leah Centre described in Chapter 1) sails into the shop, arousing the envy of the other Handmaids, and the other when Offred and Ofglen meet a group of Japanese tourists. With a shock she realises that their westernised clothes now look as exotic to her as hers do to them.

COMMENTARY

Here the important **thematic motif** of the **double** is introduced: Offred and Ofglen are doubles.

CHAPTER 6

- The Handmaids are out walking.
- They visit the Wall.
- Again Offred responds with resistance to Gilead's value system.

The walk back confirms the sinister transformation of the former university campus as the Handmaids pass the old landmarks and pause to stare at the hooded dead bodies of dissidents (doctors executed for once performing abortions) which are hanging on the Wall. Looking at the blood-stained head bag on one of the bodies with its 'red smile' (p. 43), Offred determines to try to stay sane under this tyranny by refusing to believe in the distorted versions of reality which Gilead is trying to impose.

COMMENTARY

Notice how the author powerfully builds up the sinister, repressive atmosphere during the walk back. Gilead's double image of Christianity and institutionalised oppression is confirmed in the visit to the churchyard and the Wall.

Offred's insistence on distinguishing between the significance of the colour red when it is blood and when it is the colour of flowers, along with her continuing belief in the importance of individuals despite the system, are courageous efforts to avoid confusion which

GLOSSARY

35 Libertheos Atwood's name for Central American freedom fighters, based on the concept of Liberation Theology, which has been a fashionable movement among the more politically radical Roman Catholic elements in Central and South America for the past twenty years.

35 Red Centre Rachel and Leah Re-education Centre, where Handmaids are trained (refer back to Chapter I). The name given to the Centre emphasises female sexuality.

 CHECK THE FILM
Volker Schlondorff's 1990 film of *The Handmaid's Tale* is especially good on the apparatus of the totalitarian state, though its sentimental ending falsifies the book.

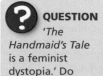 **QUESTION**
'The Handmaid's Tale is a feminist dystopia.' Do you agree?

will empower her subversive attitude throughout the novel. Her awareness of incongruities is a way of entertaining herself with language inside her head.

Section III Night

Chapter 7

- Offred has a secret escape route as she 'steps sideways' into private spaces of memory.
- Offred remembers Moira, her own mother and her lost child.

As Offred lies alone on her bed claiming that time as her own, she slips away from her real life into the past, remembering the three most influential female figures in her life in three distinctly separated scenes. There is her adolescent memory of her rebellious college friend Moira, then an earlier childhood memory of going with her mother, an early feminist activist, to a pornographic book burning which must have been in the early 1980s. Most painful of all is her agonised memory of her lost child who was taken away from her by force under the new regime, when Offred was drugged and assigned to the Red Centre to be retrained as a Handmaid.

Commentary

The focus here is on Offred's private memories as the basic technique for this survival narrative.

Offred explains that her storytelling is a survival tool. Even when she is telling the story in her head it is like a letter, a gesture toward communication with others, just as it is her only way to go on believing in a world outside the confines of Gilead.

These 'Night' episodes are the clearest evidence that this tale is a woman's narrative of resistance and survival within a system of rigid behavioural controls.

At the end of this section, we see Offred as a **self-conscious narrator** as she draws attention to her storytelling and the reasons why she needs to do it. She reveals that this is an oral narrative – 'tell rather than write' (p. 49) – so how is this story available for us to read?

SECTION IV WAITING ROOM

CHAPTER 8

- Daily life has its small surprises.
- Ofglen uses the word 'Mayday' and Offred's new Commander breaks the rules.

Daily life seems to go on as usual; only the weather changes as summer comes in. Yet Offred is alert to minor deviations from conformity. One day when they are looking at bodies on the Wall, Ofglen uses the word 'Mayday' (p. 53) – which was the standard distress call used by the Allies in the Second World War – and Offred wonders what its significance might be in Gilead. Is there a resistance movement here that she does not know about? The second oddity occurs when Offred goes upstairs after shopping and sees her new Commander peering into her room. As she passes him, he tries to look at her face. Both these acts are strictly out of order, and she is puzzled as to what they might mean.

COMMENTARY

Offred's experience is set in a social context. She notices evidence of misery and oppression all around her: in the daily executions of dissidents, the Econowives and the baby's funeral, and closer to home Serena Joy sitting alone in her garden. We learn more about Serena Joy's history and how she became a media celebrity propagandising for New Right family values. She is now a victim as Offred **satirically** remarks of the very ideology which she had formerly helped to promote.

GLOSSARY

47 **Date Rapé** (pun) compare *Fromage rapé*: grated cheese

CONTEXT

There is more evidence here of New Right family values, which criminalise any practices that interfere with sexual reproduction, abortion, homosexuality, religious vows of chastity.

GLOSSARY

53 **SOS** a Morse code distress signal, consisting of three dots, followed by three dashes, then three more dots

53 **something from Beethoven** by association, Offred thinks of the Symphony No. 5 (1807) by the German composer Ludwig von Beethoven, the famous opening phrase of which sounds like the beginning of the SOS signal

56 **Forgive them …do** Luke 23:24, Christ's words at the time of his crucifixion

? QUESTION
What are the effects of the first-person narrative on the reader of *The Handmaid's Tale*?

Going to the doctor for a compulsory monthly check-up will be the main event in this section (see Chapter 11), but 'Waiting Room' also includes other examples of 'waiting' and other examples of 'rooms'. This section underlines Gilead's objectification of women as passive sexual commodities, though 'room' also hints at the private feminine space which Offred is beginning to claim as her own inside the regime (p. 59).

CHAPTER 9

- Offred claims a room of her own.
- She discovers her unknown predecessor's secret message written in the cupboard.

Offred apparently has no control over her own life, but alone in her room, which she has begun to value as her own private space, Offred thinks back to happier times and her secret, adulterous assignations with Luke before they were married. Offred sits thinking of her unknown predecessor in this room, who left a secret message scrawled on the wall inside the closet. Though she does not know what it means, Offred keeps repeating it to herself because she is cheered by it and no longer feels so isolated. However, when she tries to find out what happened to the Handmaid before her, nobody in the house will tell her.

This is another version of her recurrent motif of **doubles** in the narrative.

GLOSSARY

62 *Nolite te bastardes carborundorum* a schoolboy Latin joke which the Commander later translates as 'Don't let the bastards grind you down'

CHAPTER 10

- In her room Offred thinks back nostalgically to her college days.
- She looks out of the window and sees Nick.

To relieve her loneliness and boredom, Offred sings snatches of hymns and old pop songs to herself (something which is now forbidden by the regime) and looks back with nostalgia to her student days of social and sexual freedom with Moira. She also remembers contemporary reports in the newspapers describing male violence against women, and begins to reassess her old attitude of social irresponsibility, wondering if such an attitude on the part of many women like herself contributed to the present loss of individual freedom in Gilead. As she turns to look out of the window, she sees Nick and the Commander getting into the car. In an upsurge of irritation she wishes she could throw a water bomb down from her window, as she and Moira used to do in their college days. Now her only recourse is to 'faith' (p. 67) which is embroidered on a cushion in her room as the other two Christian graces of 'hope' and 'charity' (or 'love') appear to be entirely absent from Gilead.

> **CONTEXT**
>
> **Faith** was one of the three primary Christian graces; see the Bible, 1 Corinthians 13:13: 'And now abideth faith, hope, charity, these three; but the greatest of these is charity.'

COMMENTARY

Faith was the cornerstone of Puritan theology, now debased by the current regime. As well as this reference to Corinthians, there is a network of allusions to 1 Corinthians 13 in the book, and it is worth noting that the two cushions with HOPE and CHARITY have disappeared. In Gilead 'hope' appears only on tombstones (see Chapter 30) and 'charity' is never mentioned except by Offred (see Chapter 19).

Offred hints at her complicated feelings for the Commander.

Offred suffers from double vision, obsessed by the contrast between her present life and her lost freedom in late twentieth-century American permissive society In this **dystopia**, 'freedom' is a forbidden word like 'hope' and 'charity'. This suggests Gilead's distortion of Christian values where hymns and popular songs are equally outlawed.

> **GLOSSARY**
>
> 64 *Amazing grace* one of the of Olney Hymns (1779) written by John Newton (1728–1807). The tune is an American folk hymn melody
>
> 64 *I feel so lonely, baby* lines from Elvis Presley's song 'Heartbreak Hotel' (1956)

CHAPTER 11

- Offred visits the doctor for her monthly check-up.
- The doctor offers to give her a baby.

At her medical check-up, Offred feels like a dismembered body with only her torso on display and her face hidden behind a paper

> **CONTEXT**
>
> This is a society where the birth rate has plummeted. This 'Birth Death' was a primary concern of the New Right, as the materials in Atwood's clippings file for the novel indicate.

screen, and the doctor himself is only partially visible, with just the upper part of his face showing above his mask.

This objectivity cracks when the doctor offers to make her pregnant, but Offred rejects this offer as being too risky. She also fears that the doctor might be a sexual exploiter and that he may be trying to coerce her into a male power game in which she would be nothing more than a collaborator and ultimately a victim.

COMMENTARY

The Handmaid's visit to the doctor is the focus of this section, with its emphasis on Gilead's essentialist definition of woman as 'two-legged wombs', but because Offred is present only as a female body to be medically checked for reproductive fitness, the chapter is deliberately kept short.

Give me children, or else I die (p. 71) is an echo of Rachel's plea in the Bible, Genesis 30:1, but it also underlines the threat to the Handmaid's life. If she fails to produce a child this time, she will be reclassified as an Unwoman and sent to the Colonies.

CHECK THE BOOK

See Atwood's exploration of sexual power politics through representations of the female body in her prose poem 'The Female Body' in *Good Bones,* pp. 39-46.

CHAPTER 12

- Offred takes a bath.
- She remembers her small daughter who was taken from her.

Back at the house, Offred prepares for the first sexual encounter with her new Commander by taking a bath. Of course, as she reflects, this is prescribed as a hygienic measure, but it is also a form of ritual purification in a society where sex is associated with sin and uncleanness.

Lying in the bath, Offred is overwhelmed by the strangeness of her own naked body and a sense of longing for her lost daughter and recalls an incident when a woman tried to steal her in a supermarket. Overwhelmed by loss, she remembers that her daughter would now be eight years old. She is, however, recalled to the present by Cora and the sight of a tattoo on her ankle. As she sits in her room waiting to be summoned, she thinks about keeping her composure, for she knows that her present social identity as Handmaid is one imposed on her, denying all her rights of choice as an individual, reducing her to passivity.

COMMENTARY

Offred is caught in the space between past and present.

Offred's final words, 'What I must present is a made thing, not something born' (p. 76), echo those of the French feminist Simone de Beauvoir in *The Second Sex* (1949): 'One is not born, but rather becomes a woman'. The art of performing femininity according to social conventions has merely taken on a different direction in Gilead.

SECTION V NAP

CHAPTER 13

- Still waiting, Offred slips away from the present into private spaces of her own body, into memory, and into dream and nightmare.
- She recalls her failed attempt to escape.

Offred describes the boredom of her situation, likening herself to 'a prize pig' (p. 79). She remembers one compulsory rest period at the Rachel and Leah Centre when her friend Moira was brought in by the Aunts, and relishes the memory of Moira's spirited resistance against the brainwashing sessions in which Janine proved herself the most abject female victim. Offred also thinks about male and female bodies, though not in the way prescribed by Gilead. Instead, she meditates intensely on her own bodily sensations.

Sinking from meditation into sleep, Offred has two of her recurring nightmares, first her dread that Luke is dead, and then her replay of their failed escape attempt across the border to Canada. There were gunshots, Luke disappeared, and Offred remembers her physical and emotional anguish as her child was dragged away from her in

GLOSSARY

74 Blessed are the meek one of the Beatitudes (see the Bible, Luke 6:20–2), describing qualities of Christian perfection

75 Four digits and an eye, a passport in reverse Gilead's tattoo which immobilises women, in contrast to the winged male eye which is the state's symbol. Compare this with the numbers tattooed on prisoners' arms in Nazi concentration camps

 QUESTION Consider the various functions of memory in relation to the representation of Offred's character and the structure of her narrative.

GLOSSARY

Les Sylphides a popular Romantic ballet, with music by Frédéric Chopin, first performed in Paris in 1909 by Diaghilev's Ballets Russes

CHECK THE BOOK

For a detailed discussion of *écriture feminine*, see Helene Cixous' essay, 'The Laugh of the Medusa' in *New French Feminisms*, 1981.

CHECK THE BOOK

Read Glenn Willmott's essay 'O Say, Can You See: *The Handmaid's Tale* as Novel and Film', where he highlights the double inauthenticity of Gilead in the representation of the Commander's household and in its television propaganda. See *Various Atwoods*, ed. Lorraine M. York, pp. 167–90.

the snow. In this state of anxiety Offred is awakened by a bell and has to leave her room to join the Commander's household downstairs.

COMMENTARY

This chapter has a very complex construction, characterised by the time shifts between present and past, and between waking and dream. The one thing Offred has in her imprisoned condition is a lot of free time, and in this waiting time she escapes her role as passive breeding animal by thinking and remembering.

When Offred is thinking about her own body it is as though she is exploring her inner space like a dark continent within her. This passage is an excellent example of *écriture feminine* where writing about her body provides the site of Offred's resistance to Gileadean ideology.

SECTION VI HOUSEHOLD

CHAPTER 14

- The Commander's household assembles for family prayers.
- In an act of resistance, Offred thinks of her own name, her first contact with Nick, her memory of her family's failed escape attempt.

The household assembles for family prayers in the sitting room. First Offred, then Cora, Rita and Nick come in, followed by the Wife, Serena Joy. The room is presided over by the Wife in her traditional space, though Offred's response to this charade of old-fashioned Puritan values is to see it as a trap like a spider's web. She emphasises its capitalist underpinnings, and mentally to compare the ageing childless Wife with the withered flowers in the vase on the table. Everyone watches the news on television and although it is only state **propaganda** we learn that Gilead is a war zone and there are religious and political prisoners and mass deportations following Gilead's racist policies.

Offred's form of private resistance is first to steal something from this room and second to think about her real name, for she holds on to that mark of her lost identity as a kind of charm in the hope that one day she will have the chance to use it again in a different future. She also recalls more of the traumatic details of her family's failed escape attempt across the border into Canada.

COMMENTARY

In this section we see Gilead's version of patriarchal authority in practice in the home. The Commander's house appears to be the embodiment of traditional family values, though Offred's account exposes this as a charade of sexual coercion, enslavement and political expediency. As Offred explains, 'Household' (p. 91) means a house and its male head: 'The house is what he holds' (p. 91); but there is also her **ironic** reference to the 'hold' (p. 91) of a ship (probably a slave ship). There is also the subtext of resistance from Nick, who touches Offred's shoe with his boot in a forbidden gesture of contact.

The domestic activities in this section show Gilead's **parody** of family values, as Offred's ironic commentaries undermine the façade of normality.

> **GLOSSARY**
>
> 91 **till death do us part** this is part of the vow in the Christian marriage service, and very threatening here, where death awaits a Handmaid if she fails to produce a child after three postings
>
> 93 **Children of Ham** and 94 **National Homeland One** references to Gilead's racist and anti-Semitic policies of forced repatriation; see the Bible, Genesis 10:6. Ham was black. Blacks are rounded up and 'resettled' in 'National Homelands', a term that recalls South African Apartheid policies

CHAPTER 15

- The Commander enters.
- There are family prayers.
- We learn of Offred's secret dissent from Gileadean orthodoxy.

Finally the Commander comes in and Offred sees him clearly for the first time as he takes the key to unlock the Bible, for he is the only person allowed to read it. In this patriarchal society only the male elite are allowed to read sacred texts. She assesses his appearance and his power, though she has her own irreverent techniques for resisting them and putting them into perspective. As the Commander drones on, reading the prescribed texts from Genesis about procreation, Offred dismisses them as 'mouldy . . . old stuff' (p. 99) and in counterpoint she thinks back to Moira's first

CONTEXT
All the following
are biblical
references: 'Be
fruitful and
multiply' (p. 99) to
Genesis 1:28; 'Give
me children' (p.
99) to Genesis
30:1–3; 'Beatitudes'
(p. 100) to
Matthew 5:3; and
'For the eyes of the
Lord' (p. 103) to
Proverbs 15:3.

attempt to escape from the Red Centre and how that time she failed and was tortured. At family prayers, Offred refuses to pray and instead she silently repeats the secret message written in her closet, linking her unknown predecessor and Moira as talismans of female resistance to Gilead's sexual tyranny.

Offred here tries to visualise what it must be like to be a man with women at his disposal, reflecting how constructions of masculinity relate to power and isolation.

Even though this is a description of family prayers, the narrator is building up the emotional tension, with the Wife's crying being treated 'like a fart in church' (p. 101) and her own irrepressible urge to laugh.

CHAPTER 16

- The impregnation ceremony takes place.
- It involves Offred, the Commander and his Wife.

The monthly impregnation ceremony ('The Ceremony') is described by Offred with deliberate detachment where she situates herself outside as 'One' (p. 106) with no hint of the personal 'I'.

Offred and Serena Joy are both there on the same bed, as Wives have to be witnesses and participants to this sexual act. Offred and the Wife are holding hands while the Commander has sex with the lower part of Offred's body. Offred reflects on the appropriate way to describe an act which is not making love nor is it rape. (Actually it is state-sanctioned rape). As the Wife, with loathing in her voice, summarily dismisses Offred from the room as soon as the Commander has 'done his duty', Offred is prompted to wonder which of the two of them suffers more.

COMMENTARY

The Ceremony is a **parodic** version of Genesis 30:1–3.

Her detailed physical description and her **ironic** comments on the Commander's performance make it plain that this is a prime example of the patriarchal oppression of women, where violation of one woman has been legitimised with another woman's complicity demanded. Yet even here Offred can see the incongruity and surreal human comedy of the situation as 'something hilarious'.

CHAPTER 17

- Offred shows her first acts of rebellion.
- She steals a flower and she embraces Nick in the sitting room in the dark.

Back in her room after the Ceremony, Offred lying in bed and 'Buttered… like a piece of toast' (p. 108) – a trick she learned at the Rachel and Leah Centre – feels restless as she gazes out at the moon and thinks of Luke, so she decides to transgress the arbitrarily imposed rules of the household by stealing something.

She goes down to the sitting room in the dark where she takes a withered daffodil from the vase, intending to press it and leave it as part of a chain of Handmaids' secret messages. It is on this occasion that she unexpectedly meets Nick, who has come to give her a different secret message from the Commander. In the dark room there is a strong sense of sexual attraction between them, all the more exciting because it is forbidden and dangerous. They embrace unexpectedly and passionately, and it is all Offred can do to drag herself away in order to stagger back quietly to her own room.

COMMENTARY

This scene is too strange and threatening to be romantic, yet the play of hands communicates mutual desire which cannot be spoken.

> **CONTEXT**
>
> Rachel and Leah were sisters who became wives of Jacob. Both gave their handmaids to him, so that he had children by all of these women. See the Bible, Genesis 29:16 and 30:1–3, 9–12.

SECTION VII NIGHT

CHAPTER 18

- Offred lies alone in bed, tormented by conflicting hopes and fears for her missing husband, Luke.
- We see the importance of hope for survival.

Back in her room and thoroughly roused, Offred remembers lying in bed with Luke before their daughter was born and contrasts this memory with her present solitary state. She tries to imagine what might have happened to Luke: is he dead, or alive in prison, or did he actually manage to escape? Kept in total ignorance and tormented by her own painful questions, all Offred can do is to hope; that is the greatest power of resistance which she has.

COMMENTARY

In this short section, the riot of images combining fear and desire where life and death are intertwined indicate Offred's tumultuous private life behind her silent, submissive exterior.

Note the intensity of the image of shattering in the first paragraph: 'this sound of glass' (p. 113). The author has built up a feeling of tremendous tension.

SECTION VIII BIRTH DAY

CHAPTER 19

- Offred dreams of her absent family and of how times once were.
- The Handmaids go out in the Birthmobile to attend the birth of Ofwarren's baby.

The chapter opens with Offred's dreams of being somewhere else with her daughter or her mother, and her desolate awakening in

QUESTION
How are the 'Night' sections different from the rest of the narrative, and what is their importance?

CONTEXT
In Gilead, reproduction defines the meaning of the Handmaids' existence as 'national resources'. Atwood's urgent warnings about pollution where human beings are at high risk of extinction provide an explanatory frame.

her room as usual. She diverts herself by thinking about words like 'chair' and 'charity' (p. 120) then eats her breakfast thinking about eggs and fertility. However, her calm is shattered by the unexpected sound of the siren of the Birthmobile, which announces that the time has come for one of the Handmaids' compulsory outings: they have to go to participate in the birth of other Handmaids' babies, and on this occasion it is Ofwarren's (Janine's). In the red truck on the way to the birth, Offred gives a frightening potted history of late twentieth-century environmental pollution and natural disasters, showing why the birth rate has plummeted, birth deformities increased and indeed why Gilead could have come about.

Guarded by soldiers with machine guns, Offred and the other Handmaids file into the home of Ofwarren's Commander and his Wife; Gilead dictates that all births should take place at home by natural childbirth methods, in the presence of women only. As Offred notes with some scepticism, Gilead's emphasis on natural childbirth embraces also the idea that the pains of childbirth are women's just punishment for Eve's Original Sin. The system also generates envy and hostility between women, keeping them divided and therefore powerless.

COMMENTARY

This section is devoted to the most significant event in the Gileadean domestic calendar, the birth of a child. Offred's account of Ofwarren's baby is a grotesquely comic mixture of birthday-party celebration and a description of natural childbirth. However, the celebrations are undermined by female rivalries, and in the rest of this section by the attempts of men and women to evade sexual coercion by the state.

CHAPTER 20

- Surrounded by other Handmaids and Wives, Offred remembers her own mother.
- She gives a brief history of the North American feminist movement.

CHECK THE BOOK

For other ecological warnings by Atwood, read 'Hardball' and 'We Want It All' in *Good Bones* (1992).

GLOSSARY

122 **San Andreas fault** a major North American earthquake zone, which runs through California. San Francisco is on this fault line

122 **Jezebels** licentious women; from the biblical story of King Ahab's heathen wife in 1 Kings 21:15. Her name appears in the Apocalypse, denoting fanaticism and profligacy (Revelations 2:20 and 17:3-5)

124 *I will greatly multiply thy sorrow* ... a reference to women's suffering in childbirth as God's punishment to Eve; see the Bible, Genesis 3:16

125 **Agent Orange** a chemical defoliant used in Vietnam by the US Airforce to remove ground cover protecting the Viet Cong, and alleged to have damaging long-term effects on humans

CHECK THE BOOK

For detailed analysis of Puritan birthing practices including the Birthing Stool, see Mark Evans's essay 'Versions of History' in *Margaret Atwood: Writing and Subjectivity* (1994).

GLOSSARY

127 **From each ... according to her ability ...** not a quotation from the Bible as the women here are told; it actually stems from a statement on capitalist methods of production made by Karl Marx (1818–83)

CHECK THE BOOK

See John Wyndham's *The Chrysalids* (1955), also a Puritan **dystopia** where deformed mutant babies are hidden or destroyed.

GLOSSARY

133 **matrix** uterus or womb (from Latin *mater*, mother)

Inside the house of Ofwarren's Commander, Offred's mind slips away from the grotesque natural childbirth performance by Janine in the master bedroom, as she remembers the Red Centre's brainwashing programmes with their films about late twentieth-century cultural history and the position of women. In one of the films Offred with a shock recognises her own young mother at one of the feminist rallies about anti-pornography and pro-abortion in the 1970s holding a banner. She thinks back to her mother's staunch feminist stance as a single parent who chooses to have a child and raise it as her own, wishing that she could have those days of comparative freedom back again.

COMMENTARY

In their combination of pornography and feminist protest, the films present an interesting, if biased, survey of sexual politics of the 1970s and 1980s.

CHAPTER 21

- Offred attends a natural childbirth.
- She muses on Gileadean transformations of the feminist phrase, 'a women's culture'.

Back in the present at the birth, Offred notices the heat and the female smells around her of sweat and blood and she chats with another Handmaid to try to find news of Moira. The baby is born and named Angela, but attention immediately switches away from the Handmaid to the Wife who will rear the child, for Janine's duty as a surrogate mother is now almost done, apart from suckling the baby for a few months.

Thinking back to her own mother, Offred realises how the feminist phrase 'a women's culture' (p. 137) has been appropriated by conservative ideology in ways her mother's generation would never have dreamed of. It is an example of the Orwellian abuses of language which characterise the official **rhetoric** of Gilead and of the frightening way that the fundamentalist Christian Right has usurped the vocabulary of radical feminism.

CHAPTER 22

- Offred returns to her room after the birth.
- She remembers the story of Moira's first heroic escape attempt from the Red Centre.

Returning home exhausted in the late afternoon, Offred tries to raise her spirits by remembering Moira's greatest act of rebellion, when she escaped from the Red Centre by tying up one of the Aunts in the basement and putting on her clothes. As an act of defiance, Moira's escape is wildly exciting to the others, but it is also frightening.

COMMENTARY

Offred clearly recognises the dangers of an absolute system of control where people quickly get used to seeing themselves as victims and begin to lose the taste of freedom.

CHECK THE BOOK
Read Atwood's 1981 Amnesty International address on the writer's moral responsibilities to bear witness, 'to retain memory and courage in the face of unspeakable suffering' in *Second Words*, pp. 393–7.

CHAPTER 23

- Offred has her first secret meeting with the Commander, where they play a forbidden game of Scrabble.
- Offred asks the question: What is 'normal' life?

By a strange juxtaposition, the same evening as the Birth Day, Offred has her first secret meeting with the Commander in his study, and it represents a radical departure from the formality of their prescribed relationship. Well aware that it is illegal and dangerous, yet unable to refuse, she is surprised to find that when she walks into the forbidden room she walks back into what used to be normal life. It is a room filled with bookcases and a sofa. The Commander's request is a strange one in the circumstances: all he wants is that Offred should play Scrabble with him, which she does. Alive to the absurdity of this, Offred wants to 'shriek with laughter' (p. 148). In the game she spells out words which refer to her own situation as a Handmaid, revelling in the forbidden privilege of

QUESTION
Look at the six words Offred chooses for the Scrabble game; can they be reconstructed as a subtext commenting on her situation as a Handmaid?

playing games with language. She finds herself feeling sorry for the Commander who, she realises, is just as isolated as she is herself.

COMMENTARY

As well as the hint of sexuality and scandal in anything forbidden, there is a strong element of narrative surprise in this chapter, which begins with another of Offred's comments on her storytelling and why it is that no story can ever recapture the whole truth of human experience. She also makes a significant comment about different kinds of power, clearly distinguishing between tyranny and the power of love and forgiveness.

SECTION IX NIGHT

CHAPTER 24

- Offred's situation changes, at least psychologically.
- She is still trapped, but now she begins to laugh at its absurdity.

CHECK THE BOOK

Linda Hutcheon's book, *The Canadian Postmodern* (1988) offers a clear analysis of the postmodern techniques of this novel in Chapter 1.

GLOSSARY

156 **Hysteria** disorder of the nervous system to which women were thought to be more liable than men. The Elizabethans thought it was caused by a disturbance of the uterus

Returning to her room, Offred thinks about her changed relationship with the Commander. With a newly awakened sense of her individuality she gives some details about herself, her age and her appearance, and her mood is much lighter. This short chapter ends with Offred's outburst of hysterical laughter. However, her situation is too precarious for her to feel carefree. She realises that she may be tempted into friendship with the Commander and remembers a television documentary she saw as a child about a Nazi war criminal's mistress who refused to believe that the man she loved was a monster, implicitly drawing a parallel between herself and that woman Of course Offred knows that she cannot laugh out loud at the absurdity of her situation, so she goes into the one hidden place in her room, into the closet where the secret message is scrawled, and there she explodes into fits of laughter. The chapter ends with the word 'opening' (p. 156).

COMMENTARY

'Context is all' (p. 154): Offred reflects on the way circumstances change her perception of the significance of events and how what is 'normal' is always a relative concept.

The word 'opening' is the signal of the end of Offred's traumatised condition and her opening out to life again.

SECTION X SOUL SCROLLS

CHAPTER 25

- High summer comes.
- Offred walks in Serena Joy's garden.
- She begins to enjoy her secret meetings with the Commander at night.

This chapter opens dramatically with 'a scream and a crash' (p. 159), for Offred has fallen asleep in the closet and Cora, the servant bringing her breakfast, thinks that Offred has killed herself like her predecessor. Offred, however, is more alive than at any point so far in the novel. High summer has come and she walks in the garden, dazzled by its beauty and giddy with desire in the midst of a pagan earthly paradise which celebrates the fecundity of nature.

Inside she is beginning to enjoy her illicit evenings in the Commander's study, where they play endless Scrabble games and he allows her to read his collection of out-of-date women's magazines (such as *Vogue* and *Ms*) while he sits watching her. Their activities would seem ordinary enough, but in Gilead they represent a breaking of taboos and a transgression of its prescribed pattern of male-female relations.

She and the Commander establish something close to an intimate relationship on very traditional lines of the eternal triangle of husband, wife and mistress. This is a pattern that is both confirmed

QUESTION
Consider the multiple meanings of Offred's outburst of laughter at the end of Chapter 24.

CHECK THE BOOK
For an analysis of Atwood as a theoretician of popular culture, see Lorna Irvine's essay, 'Recycling Culture: Kitsch, Camp and Trash in Margaret Atwood's Fiction' in R. Nischik, *Margaret Atwood: Works and Impact*, pp. 202–14.

GLOSSARY

161 **A Tennyson garden ...** *swoon*
'swoon', meaning 'to faint', occurs in the poem 'The Lotus-Eaters' (1842) by Alfred Lord Tennyson, though the garden reference points to his poem 'Maud' (1855)

and questioned when Offred asks him to get her some hand lotion, which he does. She then realises that she has nowhere to keep it, so she has to use it in the Commander's study, and he watches her putting on the lotion with all the hungry pleasure of a voyeur.

COMMENTARY

The recurrent imagery of flowers and gardens is very obvious here, where connections are made between femininity and the natural world in opposition to the polluted world of Gilead.

As the relationship with the Commander develops, Offred realises that the freedoms it brings are small, and that it is intrinsically circumscribed. Despite her pleasure in the word games she does not forget the unequal power relationship.

CHAPTER 26

- Offred attends another Ceremony.
- Her attitude shifts from detachment to emotional involvement.

Offred becomes aware of the dangers of her friendship with the Commander when the time comes around for the monthly Ceremony. She is now emotionally involved, and this inevitably complicates her relationship both with him and his Wife, for she now also takes the role of his mistress, not merely that of his Handmaid. State control cannot function if people see each other as individuals.

COMMENTARY

Through the Commander Offred is beginning to experience feelings of self-worth again.

CHAPTER 27

- Offred and Ofglen confess to each other their feelings of dissent.
- Offred discovers an underground resistance in Gilead.

Another new perspective opens up for Offred as she goes on her shopping expedition with Ofglen. Having passed the church and the Wall and the former university library, now the headquarters of the secret police, they go to stand outside 'Soul Scrolls' (p. 175), the computerised prayer factory. Here as they stare at each other's reflections in the shatterproof windows, Ofglen asks a surprising question which amounts to treason in Gilead, 'Do you think God listens... to these machines?' When Offred answers 'No' (p. 177), they both confess that they are unbelievers, and Offred discovers that Ofglen is a member of the underground Mayday resistance group. This revelation gives Offred a surge of new hope and a sense of life and hope returning as they walk back in the sunshine.

The chapter ends, however, with a sharp reminder of the power of the regime they are up against, for as they walk along they see a man being brutally beaten up by the secret police in the street and nobody dares to take any notice. Offred realises the limits of her courage when she admits to herself that she is glad she is not the victim.

COMMENTARY

In this fundamentalist state there is a vacuum at its religious centre – no public Christian worship and only mechanical repetitions of prayers. The only reality is state terrorism.

This chapter contains a dire warning about exhausting the world's natural resources – no sea fish exist any longer.

CHAPTER 28

- Offred recalls Gilead's right wing takeover of American congressional government when women were stripped of their economic, political and legal rights.
- Offred misses her husband Luke.

Offred thinks about her relationship with the Commander, and, trying to see it as Moira might have done, she realises that there are parallels to her early relation with Luke, for that too was an eternal

CHECK THE NET

The Amnesty International web site discusses human rights abuses in over 150 countries. See **http://amnesty.org**.

GLOSSARY

173 **Loaves and Fishes** for a description of Christ's miracle of the loaves and fishes, see the Bible, Mark 6:38–44

177 **Tibetan prayer wheels** cylindrical boxes inscribed with prayers, revolving on a spindle; used especially by the Buddhists of Tibet

QUESTION Using the last part of Chapter 27 as your starting point, examine the ways in which violence is presented in the novel.

CONTEXT

This account of the mechanics for a fundamentalist takeover of society speculates on the links between religious fanaticism, militarism and computerised technology. It expresses 1980s fears of the rise of the American New Right as a political force.

 CHECK THE NET

See again Atwood's interview about the novel, focusing on her prefatory note to the reader: **http://www.randomhouse.com**

triangle situation: she was his mistress before she was his wife. She recalls her joky affectionate relationship with Moira, her job in a library, and her own unquestioning acceptance of technology. She then recalls how the Gileadean regime came to power by a violent coup d'état and proceeded to implement its policies by stripping citizens of their political and legal rights. Its social policies were specifically directed against women, and married women were forcibly removed from the labour market and returned to the home in Gilead's effort to bolster the family structure for the moral good of society. What Offred remembers most clearly is her own state of shock, resentment at the loss of her economic freedom, Moira's dire warnings and her irrational anger against Luke for still having a job when hers has been taken away from her. She realises how all the advances by feminism in the 1970s and 80s for which her mother had crusaded could be swept away by simply changing computer databases. In a switch back to the present, Offred sees Nick's signal that she is to meet the Commander again and wonders what Nick thinks of the arrangement.

COMMENTARY

Most of this chapter is a **flashback**.

Note that Margaret Atwood uses the word 'job' (p. 182) to convey a number of separate ideas.

'The Book of Job' (p. 182), the Old Testament story, is, like Offred's tale, a series of catastrophes recounted by the survivors.

CHAPTER 29

- Offred asks the Commander the meaning of the Latin inscription in her room.
- She learns who wrote it and how she died.

Though the word '*Zilch*' (p. 193) betrays her real feelings, in the Commander's study Offred now feels at ease playing Scrabble and reading voraciously, and on this visit she dares to ask him the meaning of the message in her closet. When he explains that it is a schoolboy Latin joke, she realises that her predecessor must have learnt it from the Commander too and that probably her predecessor's relationship with him had been similar to her own. When he asks Offred if she would like something as a kind of payment for her time spent with him, she reveals her desire for some factual knowledge beyond the censored newscasts when she says that above all she would like to know what is going on in Gilead.

At the end of this chapter, after Offred finds out that her predecessor committed suicide when her relationship with the Commander was discovered, Offred realises that she can now play on the Commander's feelings of guilt.

COMMENTARY

Offred's asking for factual knowledge is a sign of her resistance to her marginalisation under this patriarchal rule.

SECTION XI NIGHT

CHAPTER 30

- Offred muses on a summer night.
- She longs for love, and she pours out her desperation in her version of the Lord's Prayer.

It is night again, and Offred, while gazing out of her window, happens to see Nick. Remembering their encounter in the dark sitting room, she feels the same sexual excitement and sense of frustration when a look of romantic longing is exchanged between them. Her mind flicks back from Nick to Luke and their failed escape attempt, and she realises that Luke and her daughter are beginning to seem like fading ghosts.

The chapter ends with Offred's saying the Lord's Prayer.

GLOSSARY

196 **Pen Is Envy** Red Centre motto based on Freudian psychoanalytic theory which presents 'penis envy' as an essential element of femininity, and a mark of women's natural inferiority to men

196 **Venus de Milo** a famous, now armless, statue of the goddess of love, dating from the second century BC, which is to be found in the Louvre, Paris

---

QUESTION In what sense might the Scrabble game be interpreted as a power game, or as 'kinky sex', or as a space of freedom for Offred?

QUESTION Using Offred's version of the Lord's Prayer (Chapter 30, p. 205) as a beginning, consider how religion and spiritual beliefs are presented in the novel.

CONTEXT

Of the references to Judaism on p. 211, 'the Torah' is the sacred parchment scroll on which is written the Pentateuch (first five books of the Old Testament). It is preserved in all synagogues inside the Ark of the Law, and readings from the Torah form an important part of Jewish liturgical services. 'Talliths' are rectangular prayer shawls worn by male Jews during services. 'Mogen Davids', the star of David, is composed of two equilateral overlapping triangles which form a six-pointed star. It appears on synagogues, Jewish tombstones and the Israeli flag. Gilead's raiding of synagogues replicates Nazi persecution in the Second World War.

COMMENTARY

Offred says the Lord's Prayer not in the way she was taught at the Red Centre but speaks out of her anguish in her own **ironic** version, deliberately confusing the literal and **symbolic** meanings of the words as she tries to formulate her own position. Though she tries to cling to the key Christian concepts of forgiveness and hope in the fallen world of Gilead, she is tempted to commit suicide like her predecessor. Finally she gives way to a cry of despair at her own isolation and imprisonment and her fading hopes of release. Momentarily she doubts her ability to survive the repressions of Gilead.

Compare 'Context is all; or is it ripeness?' (p. 202) with the line that appears in Shakespeare's *King Lear*, V.2: 'Ripeness is all'.

SECTION XII JEZEBEL'S

CHAPTER 31

- There is evidence of women's secret alliances in Gilead.
- We learn of Ofglen's underground resistance movement and the secret pact between Serena Joy and Offred.

Life goes on much as usual for Offred as she moves discreetly between her room and her shopping expeditions with Ofglen. Yet beneath the rules there are signs of women's resistance – not only Ofglen's secret network, but also Serena Joy's surprising offer. One day she calls Offred to her in the garden and actually suggests that she arrange for Offred to sleep with Nick in order to conceive a child without the Commander's knowledge. Offred knows she is being used, but she also recognises that Wife and Handmaid have become conspirators working in secret together to subvert Gilead's rules. To seal the bargain, Serena gives Offred an illegal cigarette and offers to let her see at last a photograph of her lost daughter. Offred almost chokes with anger that Serena Joy has kept this secret from her for so long.

COMMENTARY

This section will contain Offred's account of her night out with the Commander at Jezebel's, a high-class brothel in Gilead. The section will also include many other examples of women's exploitation by, and resistance to, the regime.

There is an extraordinary juxtaposition of locales in this section, focusing on subversive elements in Gilead: at home, at Jezebel's, at Prayvaganza, Ofglen's secret resistance network.

The phrase, 'I tell time by the moon …' (p. 209) suggests that Offred's life is regulated by menstruation – once thought to be connected with the cycle of the moon.

CHAPTER 32

- Offred considers her relationship with the Commander on the one hand, and with her hanged predecessor on the other.
- She feels afraid.

In her room, Offred does not smoke the cigarette but hoards it and the match as a secret trophy, and sits thinking about her relationship with the Commander. However, she has no doubt about her own powerlessness. She also considers his justification for Gilead's sexual laws as a puritanical response to late twentieth-century North American permissive society as well as his admission that all revolutions have their cost. When she lies down on her bed she feels more afraid than ever as she stares up at the blank space where the light fitting used to be, for she now knows why that space is blank: it was from that fitting that her predecessor hanged herself. Identifying with her, Offred has a strong sense of being stifled or already dead.

COMMENTARY

Notice how the author creates an atmosphere of claustrophobia, not only through stifling heat, but through the fact that Offred dare not voice her thoughts.

> **CONTEXT**
>
> The Commander's explanation of Gilead's ideological agenda spells out the principles of the American New Right, with its anti-feminism, its anti-homosexuality and its religious underpinnings.

CHAPTER 33

- The women's Prayvaganza: in the midst of the mass marriage celebration Offred sees Janine, one of the casualties of the system.

Offred is taken on another of the Handmaids' compulsory outings, this time to a Prayvaganza, which is a Hollywood-style extravaganza and prayer meeting to celebrate a mass wedding. This regimented affair is one of the few entertainments for women, and Offred describes it as being like a circus or a theatrical performance. Amid this public rejoicing, Offred is told by Ofglen that Janine's baby girl was destroyed because it was deformed ('a shredder' p. 226), and she remembers Janine almost having a nervous breakdown at the Red Centre, from which Moira saved her before trying to escape.

COMMENTARY

The banner, 'God is a National Resource' (p. 225) at the Prayvaganza is an example of Gilead's self-image promotion, where religion is strongly underpinned by the market values of American capitalism.

The author shows Janine as one of the casualties of the new system. Janine feels guilty at having a deformed baby, for in her world it is better to feel guilt than for life to have no meaning at all.

CHAPTER 34

- Prayvaganza celebrations are accompanied by irreverent comments from the Handmaids.
- Offglen reveals that Offred's visits to the Commander are known.

The Prayvaganza focuses on Gilead's New Right ideology as spelt out to Offred by the Commander, according to which traditional male domination over women is justified as God's law and Nature's norm. In Gilead woman is defined by her biological destiny, and

CONTEXT

The children's games on p. 224 were all common in the 1950s. In *'Do you like butter?'* buttercups were held under the chin to see their yellow reflection. In *'Blow, and you tell the time'* you puffed at dandelions gone to seed. In *'daisies for love'* you pulled off the petals and counted them to the words 'He loves me, he loves me not'.

romantic love is dismissed as a brief ripple in the history of the human race. The arranged mass marriages between soldiers and daughters of Gileadean officials provide the occasion for laying down the law on woman's subjection and silence, which is endorsed by quotations from the Bible (1 Timothy 2:9–15). But the irreverent comments by Offred and Ofglen suggest a general scepticism towards this doctrine. Ofglen reveals that Offred's secret visits to the Commander are known about and tries to recruit Offred into the resistance movement as a spy.

COMMENTARY

The author shows here that, in an authoritarian society, subversive humour is essential for those who wish to remain sane. Offred remembers with pleasure Moira's comment, 'There is a Bomb in Gilead' (p. 230) her irreverent pun on an American folk hymn, the opening words of which are: 'There is a balm in Gilead to make the wounded whole / There is a balm in Gilead to heal the sin-sick soul'. It is based on the Old Testament prophet Jeremiah's question, 'Is there no balm in Gilead; is there no physician there?' (Jeremiah 8:22). Offred delights in the exposure of Gilead's fraudulent biblical **rhetoric**.

CHECK THE BOOK

For a non-fictional critique of the dangers of contemporary consumerist society, look at Naomi Klein's book *No Logo* (2000).

CHAPTER 35

- Offred is alone in her room once again and filled with nostalgia for the outmoded habit of falling in love.
- Serena brings the borrowed photograph of Offred's daughter.

Back in her room again, Offred fills her blank time by remembering her family's failed escape attempt and thinking of the one element that the Prayvaganza left out of the marriage service: sexual love. She has a long nostalgic digression on 'falling in love' which she is old enough to remember having done herself many times, though her central focus is on Luke.

Her reverie is interrupted by Serena Joy, who appears with the photograph of Offred's daughter. For Offred, however, this is a new source of grief, since she thinks that she will have been forgotten by

GLOSSARY

237 **That word, made flesh** (pun) 'the Word made flesh', see the Bible, John 1:14

239 **White Russian drinking tea in Paris** aristocratic refugees from the Russian Revolution in 1917 went into exile throughout Europe and there were a large number of them in Paris in the 1920s. They were known as 'white Russians' because they opposed the Red Army of the Bolsheviks

her daughter, just as she will be forgotten when the history of Gilead is written.

COMMENTARY

In Offred's reveries about falling in love, she is continually seeing the present through her memories of the past and judging it according to former values.

CHAPTER 36

QUESTION
Analyse the narrative significance of the variety of devices used in this novel: the single photograph, the cassette recordings at the end, news bulletins, Red Centre cinema and Offred's metaphorical letters.

- Offred has a surprise evening out with the Commander.
- She dresses up, as for a masquerade party.

The Commander breaks all the rules by inviting Offred to dress up and go out with him one evening. It is a bizarre enterprise as well as a dangerous one, but Offred accepts, partly because she cannot refuse and partly because she craves some excitement. The Commander produces an old purple satin costume with feathers and sequins plus high-heeled shoes, and he even supplies the make-up and a mirror and a blue cloak which he has borrowed secretly from his Wife. This is an **irony** not lost upon Offred, who sees herself now as Serena's double. Her wry self-description makes it plain that her costume is a **parody** of feminine glamour.

It is Nick who has to drive them on this clandestine outing, but Offred cannot tell whether he approves or disapproves of what she is doing. As they drive down a back alley and hurry through a dark entrance, Offred is left in no doubt of the Commander's attitude nor of her status in this enterprise, for he ties a label on her wrist and steers her in as if she were an object which he has won or perhaps just rented for the evening.

COMMENTARY

Offred's treat does not appear to bring her new status. Though dressed, at the outset, as a Wife, she is soon asked to play the role of 'an evening rental' (p. 245) or prostitute.

CHAPTER 37

- Jezebel's turns out to be the state brothel, Gilead's sexual underground.
- We glimpse its male clientèle and the women who work there.
- Offred meets Moira again.

The place to which the Commander takes Offred is familiar to her because it turns out to be the hotel where she had formerly come with Luke during their affair, but the scenario is oddly unfamiliar, for it is like a film, not real life. Forbidden under Gilead's Puritanical rules, the place is nevertheless run by the state as a brothel for officers and foreign trade delegations, and what it represents are pornographic male fantasies about women. There are women dressed up in Bunny Girl costumes or like devils and *femmes fatales*; everything is entirely focused on male fantasy and desire. These women are here because they refused to be assimilated as Handmaids, and their only alternative to being sent to the Colonies was to join the staff at the brothel. They are 'professionals' (both in the sense of professional career women and in the sense of prostitutes) but officially they do not exist. They are not 'people' but sexual objects available for rent.

Offred suddenly sees Moira, in an outfit even more grotesque than her own. By their old secret signal they agree to meet in the women's washroom, and Offred excuses herself from the Commander, leaving him sipping his drink in the lounge.

COMMENTARY

'Jezebel's' is an episode which is both comic and bleak.

There is a **paradox** here: it may appear that the Commander is taking Offred out to give her a feeling of freedom, but he takes her to a place where women are at their most debased. However, Offred does get a glimpse of freedom, **symbolised** by Moira, and her main interest is in this alternative women's society within Gilead.

CONTEXT

Jezebel's is named after the wicked scarlet woman in the Bible, and so represents the hypocrisy and sexism which characterises the military dictatorship of Gilead.

CHAPTER 38

- At Jezebel's Moira tells Offred about her failed escape attempt and how she came to be working in the brothel.
- Offred reflects on Moira's unfinished story.

In the washroom, presided over by an Aunt disguised as a Madame, Offred and Moira manage to tell each other what has happened to them since Moira's escape from the Red Centre. Of course it is Moira who suggests that the Commander brought Offred to Jezebel's as part of a male power fantasy, and there is plenty of evidence for this feminist analysis.

COMMENTARY

Offred embeds the story of Moira's escape attempt inside her own narrative, partly to celebrate Moira's heroism and that of all the people who helped her get as far as the Canadian border, but partly as an elegy to Moira whom Offred will never see again after tonight.

In this chapter feminism and religious fundamentalism are held together in tension. There is focus on sexual politics and power games.

The sad truth is that Moira has not managed to escape from Gilead any more than Offred's unknown predecessor; the most that Offred can do if she survives is to tell their stories of resistance.

CHAPTER 39

- In a bedroom at Jezebel's, the Commander arranges a private sexual encounter with Offred.
- It is a dismal failure.

The Commander takes Offred upstairs for what he assumes will be a pleasurable sexual encounter for them both, but it is doomed to failure. A private relationship between Offred and the Commander is not possible, there are too many memories of Luke in the hotel, and Offred also remembers Moira's account of her mother being sent to the Colonies by the Gileadean regime. Consequently she does not want to see him as a naked human being and would prefer the grotesque arrangement with Serena Joy present as well. In bed she feels she has to pretend to enjoy it, both for the Commander's sake and for her own safety, but the encounter is a dismal failure.

COMMENTARY

No private relationship between Offred and the Commander is possible, for the personal has become inescapably political.

Offred cannot forget that the Commander represents the tyrannical power which is responsible for her losses and that she is his slave, emphasised by her self-admonishment, '**Move your flesh around**' (p. 267).

SECTION XIII NIGHT

CHAPTER 40

- Offred has her first sexual encounter with Nick.
- She falls in love with him.

Although she knows she is still being used, this time by the Commander's Wife, Offred's encounter with Nick is entirely different and her account of their first lovemaking is curiously reticent about what really happened. In this precarious situation there is for Offred a further problem of her infidelity to Luke and her ignorance about his fate, all of which is part of the dilemma of human love explored by Offred in her narrative as she tries to maintain her integrity in the face of uncertainty, deprivation and desire.

COMMENTARY

The plot takes a new turn. By contrast to the last chapter, this one describes Offred's romantic love affair with Nick.

QUESTION How does the love story between Offred and Nick both conform to and parody the conventional True Romance plot?

She tries to tell it in three different ways, but she admits that none of them is true because no language can adequately describe the complex experience of falling in love. These multiple versions are also a reminder of Offred's self-consciousness as a narrator, who creates different effects through her way of telling the story.

Falling in love is for Offred an act of survival and resistance in Gilead.

SECTION XIV SALVAGING

CHAPTER 41

- Offred's risky love affair with Nick defies Gileadean tyranny.
- For the first time, she wants to stay in Gilead.

CONTEXT

The word 'Salvaging' has associations with 'salvage', 'salvation' and 'savage'. Elsewhere Atwood has commented that in the Philippines 'salvaging' has now come to mean 'public execution', a startling example of the abuse of language. This section indicates the dangers of disobeying the law in Gilead.

Offred continues her love affair with Nick. She is totally compromised not only in relation to her memories of Luke, but in her official relation with the Commander and her unofficial relation with Ofglen's resistance movement. She is also in danger of being shot by mistake in the dark. Yet to her, being in love again is like a refuge in the wilderness, and she abandons herself to this crucial human emotion which Gilead cannot wipe out. She shows how much she trusts Nick by telling him her real name. For the first time she actually wants to stay in Gilead, as long as she can be with Nick.

COMMENTARY

Perhaps to underline the precariousness of her illicit love affair with Nick, Offred embeds it in this most gruesome section of the novel, in which she describes a public execution and an outbreak of mob violence. Offred begins by speculating once more on the function of her narrative, which works both as an eye-witness account and as a substitute for dialogue. Addressing her imaginary reader, she warns that this next part of her story does her no credit, but she is determined to try to tell the truth as she feels that her reader deserves it. The love scenes with Nick are both ambiguous and tender.

CHAPTER 42

- At the Salvaging two Handmaids and one Wife are publicly hanged.
- Offred cannot look.

The Salvaging is another compulsory outing, this time to witness the execution of two Handmaids and one Wife. Again it is a showbiz event, set outside on the lawn in front of what was once the university library, and it reminds Offred of a graduation ceremony until the proceedings begin. It is not, however, even a show trial, for the women are hanged for unspecified crimes. It is a frightening display of fanaticism presided over by Aunt Lydia in which all Handmaids are forced to become collaborators, for they all have to put their hands on the hanging rope to signify their assent to these killings.

COMMENTARY

The chilling violence of the Salvaging reminds us of the precariousness of Offred's illicit affair with Nick.

CHAPTER 43

- At a Particicution, a man accused of rape is torn to pieces by the mob of outraged Handmaids.
- Offglen tells Offred that he was no rapist, but a dissenter like themselves.

The Salvaging reaches a horrendous climax in the public slaughter of a man supposed to have been convicted of rape. This 'Particicution' is a dreadful spectacle of female violence, for it is the Handmaids who are encouraged to kill and dismember him. It is conducted by Aunt Lydia who blows a whistle as in a football game. Everyone is overcome by a wave of hysteria and revenge, though Offred notices that the man tries to smile and to deny the charge. Ofglen rushes forward and kicks the man to knock him out before he is torn to

CONTEXT

Atwood's 'I tell, therefore you are' (p. 279) is a punning variation of René Descartes' 'Cogito ergo sum' ('I think, therefore I am') from his *Discourse on Method* (1637), where he defines thought as the essential characteristic of a human being. Atwood's version emphasises language and communication rather than the self-enclosed mind.

CHECK THE FILM

The horror of this episode is vividly portrayed in Volker Schlondorff's 1990 film, and also in Paul Ruder's opera of *The Handmaid's Tale*, first performed in Copenhagen, 2001 and in London, 2003.

CHECK THE BOOK

George Orwell's *Nineteen Eighty-Four* with its organised 'Two minutes Hate' is an important model for the mass hysteria and cruelty of the Particicution.

GLOSSARY

289 **a kind of dance** this recalls the film *The Red Shoes* (1948), starring Moira Shearer as the ballerina who danced herself to death

290 **Particicution** the word combines 'participation' (by the Handmaids) and 'execution' (of the victim)

290 **Deuteronomy 22:23–29** Gilead follows the Old Testament law that the penalty for rape is death

pieces, and the chapter ends with Ofglen telling Offred that the man was not a rapist but a member of the resistance movement. Then Janine appears with a smear of blood across her cheek as she drifts away into madness. Offred's own reaction makes her extremely uncomfortable, for the man's terrible death has acted on her like a stimulant, enhancing her own sense of physical survival.

COMMENTARY

Among other things, the author is showing us the brutalising effects of crowd hysteria.

CHAPTER 44

- Offred's normal life is shattered by the disappearance of Ofglen.
- She is told that Ofglen has hanged herself.

Later that same afternoon when Offred goes shopping, thinking that things have returned to what is normal in Gilead, she is astonished to find that she has a different partner and her friend Ofglen has been replaced by someone else (who is now 'Ofglen'). Again Offred feels the threat of risk but cannot contain her curiosity about her friend. She is even more astonished to be told that the former Ofglen hanged herself after the Salvaging because she saw the black truck coming for her.

COMMENTARY

The author has created a feeling of extreme tension here, where not knowing is more frightening than knowing.

CHAPTER 45

- Offred suffers her worst crisis of despair.
- Serena Joy reveals that she knows about Offred's clandestine evening with the Commander.

The knowledge that Ofglen committed suicide before she could be made to confess and endanger her friends in the resistance brings Offred to her worst crisis of despair. She finds that she is prepared to accept survival at any price and feels for the first time that she has been defeated and overpowered by Gilead. This is also the moment when Serena Joy confronts her with a more personal betrayal, holding out the cloak and the purple costume as evidence of her evening out with the Commander. She also tells Offred that what she did was what her predecessor had done, and that she will meet the same fate. Offred can do nothing except go up to her room alone.

CHECK THE FILM

Things to Come (1936) scripted by H. G. Wells is the classic futuristic dystopia, offering a masculine perspective on history which is vast and chilling.

COMMENTARY

Offred's decision to stop fighting brings with it a feeling of relief, only to be snatched away by the Wife's revelation. The plot now gathers pace; it seems to be moving towards a dénouement.

SECTION XV NIGHT

CHAPTER 46

- This is Offred's last crisis.
- There is a surprising twist in the plot, and she makes her exit.

Offred sits in her room in a state of torpid indifference while she considers a variety of possible escapes, but does nothing. This is her worst moment of total despair when she feels as trapped as her predecessor, whose defiance ended in suicide. In fact Offred confirms the **thematic motif** of the **double** when she says, 'There were always two of us' (p. 305). Then comes a break in the text and an astonishing intervention, for suddenly Offred hears the siren of the black van and a group of Eyes led by Nick push open her door. Offred fears that Nick has betrayed her and she is immediately on the defensive, ready to accuse him. However, he whispers that this is Mayday come to her rescue and more significantly he calls her by her real name. This secret which Offred has told him during their lovemaking would seem to be a coded message of reassurance to Offred and to the reader. It is the only hope that she or we have to cling to.

CONTEXT

The coming of the van, the uncertainty of Offred's destination are echoes of life in any totalitarian regime, from Stalinist Russia and Nazi Germany to apartheid South Africa and the 'disappearances' under the military juntas of Chile and Argentina.

CHECK THE NET

For specifically Canadian environmental issues, see Greenpeace Canada: http://www.greenpeace.ca.

So Offred departs from the Commander's house, escorted out by the Eyes like a criminal and ridden with guilt at having let down everyone in the household, who all stand gaping at her in disbelief. Offred has no idea whether she is about to go to prison or to freedom, but she allows herself to be helped up into the van. In the midst of her uncertainty and powerlessness it is a final gesture of trust and faith, confirmed perhaps by the final words of the novel when light succeeds darkness: 'And so I step up, into the darkness within, or else the light' (p. 307).

COMMENTARY

This last chapter is very dramatic, both in the sense of being similar to a play (or a melodrama as Offred calls it) with Offred as the character centre stage, and in terms of the surprise twist of the ending as she makes her exit from the novel.

HISTORICAL NOTES

HISTORICAL NOTES ON *THE HANDMAID'S TALE*

- There is a flash forward to AD 2195, where at an academic conference Offred's tale is presented as a historical curiosity.
- Her fate remains a mystery and Gilead has long since disappeared.

These Notes are a supplement to the story we have just finished reading and they provide a framework for looking back at Offred's narrative from a distant point in the future when Gilead is in ruins and all the protagonists of the story are dead. It is also a view from outside the United States, for this conference paper is being given at a Symposium on Gileadean Studies in Arctic Canada by a male archivist from the University of Cambridge, England. The session is chaired by a woman professor whose name, Maryann Crescent Moon, suggests that she is a member of the Native peoples (like her colleague, Professor Running Dog) who are now evidently in charge of their own educational policies.

As well as providing necessary background information, the Notes tell us how Offred's story has survived and why its structure is so fragmented. It was not written down but recorded on cassette tapes which were unearthed on the site of the ruined city of Bangor, Maine. It is a transcription of these tapes, discovered and edited by two Cambridge professors, which we have been reading.

Professor Pieixoto cannot identify Offred, partly because her real name was already obscured by the Gileadean patronymic and partly because he spends most of his time trying to identify her Commander whose name was probably a pseudonym. He is really much more interested in pursuing an 'objective' view of history and in analysing Gileadean social theory in a broadly historical context. For all his scholarship he cannot get beyond generalities and fails to tell us what we most want to know, that is, what happened to Offred.

COMMENTARY

This is the last 'reconstruction' of Offred's tale, and incidentally a sharply **satirical** attack on the methodology and manners of male academic historians. The Notes alter our perspective on Offred, for here she is no longer a living, suffering human being but an elusive anonymous voice whose story is nothing more than an anecdote in ancient history. The professor likens her to Eurydice who in Greek mythology was the wife of Orpheus. He rescued her from Hades, but when he looked back to see if she was following, she vanished for ever. As readers, we may well object to this distancing technique, which is as reductive of Offred's identity as Gilead's depersonalising of her as one of its Handmaids. We are likely to feel that his historical interpretation misses the point, and that, **ironically**, his only useful role is as a male Handmaid who has succeeded in bringing Offred's tale to light. If we see the tale as a letter, it is he who finally delivers the message, through transforming 'herstory' back into 'history' in the process. However we may be thankful for his scholarly endeavours as, through them, her tale has survived, so that now at last Offred can speak for herself. The final question invites us as readers to participate in interpreting the multiple and contradictory meanings of what we have just finished reading.

CHECK THE BOOK

Read Atwood's poems 'Orpheus' 1 and 2, and 'Eurydice', first published in 1984 and collected in her *Eating Fire: Selected Poetry 1965–1995*.

CONTEXT

Musical references on p. 314 set Offred's story in the 'past'. 'Elvis Presley's Golden Years' is an album of the American rock and roll singer's best songs, recorded in 1964. 'Folk Songs from Lithuania' is an example of mid-1980s 'Roots Revolution' ethnic songs. 'Boy George Takes It Off' is a deliberately provocative album by the gay British pop singer, George O'Dowd (b. 1961), made in the mid-1980s. 'Mantovani's Mellow Strings' was popular orchestral music in the early 1960s, and this recording was made in 1961. 'Twisted Sister at Carnegie Hall' is a tape of a live show by this mid-1980s Californian rock group, whose male lead singer dressed in women's clothes.

GLOSSARY

312 **Krishna and Kali Elements** in Hindu mythology; Krishna is the most benign of the gods and Kali is the ferocious goddess of death and destruction

312 **Sumptuary Laws** laws regulating expenditure, especially with a view to restraining excess spending on food or equipment

312 **Arctic Char** a salmon-like fish found in the North West Territories, which is an important source of food and income for the Inuits

312 **'enjoy'... the obsolete third** sense of the word is 'to have sexual relations with a woman'

313 **Geoffrey Chaucer** his *Canterbury Tales* (c. 1387) include two women's tales, by the 'Wife of Bath' and the 'Prioress', one emphasising sexual love and the other spiritual love

313 *tail* the pun refers to American slang for a woman reduced to her sexual function, for example, 'a nice bit of tail'

EXTENDED COMMENTARIES

In the 'Historical Notes' Professor Pieixoto criticises Offred's account: 'She could have told us much about the workings of the Gileadean empire, had she had the instincts of a reporter or a spy' (p. 322). Offred does have these instincts, but she chooses to report not on public but on private matters. The four passages chosen for textual analysis are examples of her counter-discourse which challenges Gilead's patriarchal narrative. They are also important for discussing language, narrative technique and key themes in the novel as a whole, and the commentary will refer to these topics.

TEXT 1 – CHAPTER 5 (PAGE 33)

Doubled, I walk the street. Though we are no longer in the Commanders' compound, there are large houses here also. In front of one of them a Guardian is mowing the lawn. The lawns are tidy, the façades are gracious, in good repair; they're like the beautiful pictures they used to print in the magazines about homes and gardens and interior decoration. There is the same absence of people, the same air of being asleep. The street is almost like a museum, or a street in a model town constructed to show the way people used to live. As in those pictures, those museums, those model towns, there are no children.

This is the heart of Gilead, where the war cannot intrude except on television. Where the edges are we aren't sure, they vary, according to the attacks and counterattacks; but this is the centre, where nothing moves. The Republic of Gilead, said Aunt Lydia, knows no bounds. Gilead is within you.

Doctors lived here once, lawyers, university professors. There are no lawyers any more, and the university is closed.

Luke and I used to walk together, sometimes, along these streets. We used to talk about buying a house like one of these, an old big house, fixing it up. We would have a garden, swings for the children. We would have children. Although we knew it wasn't too likely we could ever afford it, it was something to talk about, a game for Sundays. Such freedom now seems almost weightless.

This is Offred's account of going out to do the daily shopping with her new partner, another Handmaid named Ofglen. Under the Gileadean regime Handmaids never went out unaccompanied, the partnership system providing both chaperones and spies. Offred considers this image of two women dressed identically in red, thinking of them as twins both visually and in circumstances: 'Doubled, I walk the street.' The Handmaids seem like the personification of feminine submissiveness and companionship. However, as she reflects, this is in appearance only, for the Handmaids are a parody of femininity, acting out a masquerade which hides Gilead's oppression of women. These scarlet women are classified as 'sacred vessels' (p. 146) or sisters, 'dipped in blood' (p. 19), incarnating Gilead's fascination with and vilification of female sexuality.

This first sentence is also a striking introduction to the motif of **doubles**, which appears throughout the novel. Offred has other doubles as well as Ofglen, such as her predecessor who hanged herself in the cupboard of the room which she now occupies, and there is the Commander's Wife whose blue cloak was part of Offred's disguise when she went to Jezebel's with the Commander and with whom she shares the Commander's sexual attentions. There is also Janine (Ofwarren), a kind of dark double, who represents what Offred might have become if she had allowed herself to be brainwashed by Gilead. The common thematic element that unites these women is that they are all oppressed by the same patriarchal regime.

Walking along the suburban street, Offred thinks about the houses and gardens she passes, for though they are well kept there is something artificial about this scenario: it is empty, museum-like, for there are no people and certainly no children, in itself a signal of the crisis at the centre of Gilead's social and political life. What Offred remarks on is the **parody** of family life which is on display in Gilead's public spaces, similar to the private spaces of the Commander's household. At the heart of Gilead there is not peace, but the illusion of peace, as Offred had remarked on seeing the Wife in her garden earlier that day: 'From a distance it looks like peace' (p. 22).

CHECK THE BOOK

See Lynette Hunter, '"That will never do": Public History and Private Memory in *Nineteen Eighty-Four* and *The Handmaid's Tale*' in: *Lire Margaret Atwood: The Handmaid's Tale*, ed. M. Dvorak, for a discussion of gender difference in the treatment of topics like history, memory and sexuality.

CHECK THE BOOK

For a detailed analysis of how Offred's interior monologue gives us information both public and private about normal life in the 'time before', see Lee Briscoe Thompson, *Scarlet Letters*, pp. 57–7.

QUESTION

Consider the importance of the recurrent motif of doubles in this novel.

Offred exposes this false image of domestic security as nothing but dead space 'where nothing moves,' and this is amplified in her comments on the difference between centres and borders. Just as the edges of the embattled state are continually shifting, so the limits of Gilead's power are ill-defined. The regime's **propaganda** encourages the terrifying possibility that Gilead is not just a territorial state but also a state of mind. As Aunt Lydia has told the women at the Red Centre, 'Gilead is within you' (p. 33), which is the ultimate in a brainwashing programme where all the doctrines of the state are internalised by its citizens. This pronouncement is both legitimated and made more horrifying by its blasphemous appropriation of the biblical promise: 'The Kingdom of God is within you.'

As Offred walks along, ostensibly in a pair but really locked into isolation, her survival strategies come into play. She remembers what this locality was like in 'the time before' when this was a professional middle-class neighbourhood, though now all the 'Doctors… lawyers, university professors' have vanished along with their jobs. She does not say who lives in these houses under the new regime (possibly she does not know), but we assume they have been requisitioned by the state and reallocated.

In a characteristic shift in mental perspective via association with place, Offred's memories of this street are superimposed over Gilead's charade of normality, as she escapes into her own private narrative of vanished Sunday walks with her lost husband. She remembers their domestic aspirations to buy a big house and garden in which to live as a family with those children whose absence makes the streets so dead in the present. This is her silent discourse of resistance to everything Gilead stands for and has done to her, just as it is an exposure of the hypocrisy of the regime. More importantly, Offred's memory narrative celebrates her ordinary humanity while it reassures her and the reader that she preserves her secret identity (like her 'shining name' (p.94) underneath her imprisoning Handmaid's costume whose heaviness contrasts with her recollections of 'weightless' freedom in the past.

> **CONTEXT**
>
> Spatial and temporal dislocations registered in Offred's private narrative represent her most important escape mechanisms so that her restricted Handmaid's space expands into spaces of memory and desire.

TEXT 2 – CHAPTER 13 (PAGES 83–4)

I sink down into my body as into a swamp, fenland, where only I know the footing. Treacherous ground, my own territory. I become the earth I set my ear against, for rumours of the future. Each twinge, each murmur of slight pain, ripples of sloughed-off matter, swellings and diminishings of tissue, the droolings of the flesh, these are signs, these are the things I need to know about. Each month I watch for blood, fearfully, for when it comes it means failure. I have failed once again to fulfill the expectations of others, which have become my own.

I used to think of my body as an instrument, of pleasure, or a means of transportation, or an implement for the accomplishment of my will. I could use it to run, push buttons, of one sort or another, make things happen. There were limits but my body was nevertheless lithe, single, solid, one with me.

Now the flesh arranges itself differently. I'm a cloud, congealed around a central object, the shape of a pear, which is hard and more real than I am and glows red within its translucent wrapping. Inside it is a space, huge as the sky at night and dark and curved like that, though black-red rather than black. Pinpoints of light swell, sparkle, burst and shrivel within it, countless as stars. Every month there is a moon, gigantic, round, heavy, an omen. It transits, pauses, continues on and passes out of sight, and I see despair coming towards me like famine. To feel that empty, again, again. I listen to my heart, wave upon wave, salty and red, continuing on and on, marking time.

Offred's role as Handmaid defines her in biological terms as a breeder, a **'two-legged womb'** (p. 146). Yet she manages to survive psychologically and emotionally by resisting Gilead's definition as she writes about her body in terms significantly different from patriarchal prescriptions. In this remarkable passage on the evening of the monthly Ceremony (when her body would seem least of all to be her own), Offred refuses to be subjugated by the Commander's violation and instead she becomes the explorer of her own dark inner space. Offred insists on chronicling her life from within her own skin, offering her personal history of physical sensations, though the imagery she uses transforms her body into a fantasy landscape. She imagines it first as an unknown continent which she is trying to map, and later as a cosmic wilderness. To describe the rhythms of her menstrual cycle she uses the image of

> **? QUESTION**
> Compare representations of the female body in Chapters 11, 12 and 13.

the night sky studded with stars and traversed by the moon waxing and waning. Accurate in every detail as **analogy**, this is also a transforming **metaphor**, as the dark womb space expands until it assumes cosmic proportions. When the moon disappears, leaving the sky empty, Offred, not having conceived, is also left empty and drained of hope. The only issue will be blood, whose rhythm she feels beating through her like the sea, for this is her own dark female space where time is kept by the body: 'I tell time by the moon. Lunar, not solar' (p. 209). This passage also makes an allusion to the connections between the cycle of the moon, the menstrual cycle, and the ebb and flow of the tides.

With her close attention to physical details, Offred not only charts her bodily awareness but also her changing sense of herself under the influence of Gilead's cultural doctrines. She notes that she no longer thinks of her body as a 'solid' object and the agent of her own will, but instead she has learned to think of it as a 'cloud' of flesh surrounding her womb which has become her most important physical feature. Her position is one of compromised resistance where she is very much affected by her material circumstances: she both resents Gilead's control over her and yet regrets not becoming pregnant as the system requires of her. She wonders how long she will survive, for 'marking time' reminds her that time is running out and she will be sent to the Colonies if she does not soon produce a child. Despite her anxieties, in her mind her body remains unconquered territory which will be forever beyond the Commander's reach. Through metaphor Offred resists Gilead's appropriation of her body. She also offers an alternative imaginary landscape to the night sky of Gilead streaked with searchlights, where her images of immense bodily territories and the later volcanic upheaval of her silent laughter in the cupboard (Chapter 24) have much in common with the *écriture feminine* (feminine writing) of the French feminist theorist Hélène Cixous.

TEXT 3 – CHAPTER 25 (PAGES 161–2)

Well. Then we had the irises, rising beautiful and cool on their tall stalks, like blown glass, like pastel water momentarily frozen in a splash, light blue, light mauve, and the darker ones, velvet and purple, black cat's-ears in the sun, indigo shadow, and the bleeding hearts, so female in shape it was a surprise they'd not

---

CONTEXT

Hélène Cixous' essay 'The Laugh of the Medusa' urges women to write in a new way about their personal experience, using the imagery of body sensations and emotional rhythms, just as Atwood is doing here

---

long since been rooted out. There is something subversive about this garden of Serena's, a sense of buried things bursting upwards, wordlessly, into the light, as if to point, to say: Whatever is silenced will clamour to be heard, though silently. A Tennyson garden, heavy with scent, languid; the return of the word *swoon*. Light pours down upon it from the sun, true, but also heat rises, from the flowers themselves, you can feel it: like holding your hand an inch above an arm, a shoulder. It breathes, in the warmth, breathing itself in. To walk through it in these days, of peonies, of pinks and carnations, makes my head swim.

The willow is in full plumage and is no help, with its insinuating whispers. *Rendezvous*, it says, *terraces*; the sibilants run up my spine, a shiver as if in fever. The summer dress rustles against the flesh of my thighs, the grass grows underfoot, at the edges of my eyes there are movements, in the branches; feathers, flittings, grace notes, tree into bird, metamorphosis run wild. Goddesses are possible now and the air suffuses with desire. Even the bricks of the house are softening, becoming tactile; if I leaned against them they'd be warm and yielding. It's amazing what denial can do. Did the sight of my ankle make him lightheaded, faint, at the check-point yesterday, when I dropped my pass and let him pick it up for me? No handkerchief, no fan, I use what's handy.

Winter is not so dangerous. I need hardness, cold, rigidity; not this heaviness, as if I'm a melon on a stem, this liquid ripeness.

This passage offers a complex representation of Offred as heroine: she pictures herself as heroine of romance, though through her imaginative celebration of natural beauty and fertility she shows heroic resistance to being subjugated by Gilead's sterile patriarchal power. In the grim circumstances of Gilead Offred still manages to believe in love and desire and the delights of the flesh. As she says when commenting on her story, 'I've tried to put some of the good things in as well. Flowers, for instance' (p. 279). She is particularly attracted to the Commander's Wife's garden, which, though it is enclosed by a brick wall and not available to her to sit in, represents a different space outside. She is fascinated by the garden as an image of the natural world which celebrates the beauty and fertility already lost in the public world of Gilead and reminds her of her

> **CONTEXT**
> Alfred, Lord Tennyson (1809-92) wrote some of the most sensuous and atmospheric poetry about gardens in the Victorian era. Look at *Maud* (1855): '...the woodbine spices are wafted abroad,/And the musk of the rose is blown...' and *The Princess*: (1847): 'Now sleeps the crimson petal...'

own garden in her past life (Chapter 3). When she talks about the garden she always says 'we' and 'our', signalling her private sense of possessing its beauty. This is the one spot in the household where she feels a strong sense of belonging. In this lyrical passage Offred rhapsodises over the summer garden in full bloom, finding in it a moment of release when she transcends her physical constraints and enters into the otherness of the natural world. The flower imagery with its sexual suggestiveness provides an image of her own repressed desires, but more than that, the garden becomes suddenly the space of romantic fantasy, 'a Tennyson garden', 'the return of the word *swoon*', where traditional images of femininity breathe through the prose as the garden itself 'breathes' in the light and heat of summer.

Offred experiences the garden as a place of living colour and movement, a place of delightful temptation, where she hears the willow tree whispering its promises of romantic trysts. In this world of heightened physical sensation she becomes aware of her own body inside her red dress, with the same sensitivity as she feels the grass growing and hears the birds singing. The dynamic natural rhythms are so powerful that she imagines that she is actually observing the process of 'metamorphosis' in which things change from one shape into another, so that the rustling leaves and fluttering birds merge together and the tree becomes the bird 'in full plumage'. In her mind this process is associated with Ovid's *Metamorphoses*, the early first-century Latin poem about supernatural transformations of human beings into trees or animals. The word 'goddesses' focuses images of myth and desire, and as Offred watches, everything comes alive, even the brick walls which become soft and warm like flesh. Of course Offred suspects that her rhapsody is at least in part a sublimation of her own frustrated desires, and she remembers the way in which she teased the young guard who was on duty the day before, wryly admitting the limited props available for her short flirtatious scenario.

CONTEXT

The *Metamorphoses*, like the *Iliad* and the *Odyssey*, represent the Classical heritage of Western literature. The key factor for Offred is that these poems are pagan and pastoral in opposition to Gilead's biblical rhetoric.

This garden is represented as a feminised emblem of sexual desire. Offred's imagination is not attached to the Christian image of the enclosed paradise presided over by the Virgin Mary as the image of female virtue, even though Serena Joy, whose garden it is, wears a blue gardening dress, the Virgin's colour. Instead, for Offred it is a pagan garden presided over by goddesses, and being in the garden evokes a heady combination of feelings filtered through a literary imagination which enacts its own magical transformations. It is a kind of nature mysticism where Offred herself undergoes a 'metamorphosis', changing from Handmaid to ripening fruit like a 'melon on a stem' attached to a natural life-giving source, as she becomes for a moment a part of this pulsating world filled with a yearning for love and the energy of desire. This extract shows Offred's characteristic mixture of lyricism and **irony**, for she knows that this erotic fantasising is an escape from her real circumstances which are bleak and deathly as winter. However, her impressive energy defies Gilead's master narrative of phallic power underpinned by the Bible.

TEXT 4 – CHAPTER 41 (PAGES 279–80)

I wish this story were different. I wish it were more civilized. I wish it showed me in a better light, if not happier, then at least more active, less hesitant, less distracted by trivia. I wish it had more shape. I wish it were about love, or about sudden realizations important to one's life, or even about sunsets, birds, rainstorms, or snow.

Maybe it is about those things, in a sense; but in the meantime there is so much else getting in the way, so much whispering, so much speculation about others, so much gossip that cannot be verified, so many unsaid words, so much creeping about and secrecy. And there is so much time to be endured, time heavy as fried food or thick fog; and then all at once these red events, like explosions, on streets otherwise decorous and matronly and somnambulent.

I'm sorry there is so much pain in this story. I'm sorry it's in fragments, like a body caught in crossfire or pulled apart by force. But there is nothing I can do to change it.

I've tried to put some of the good things in as well. Flowers, for instance, because where would we be without them?

Nevertheless it hurts me to tell it over, over again. Once was enough: wasn't once enough for me at the time? But I keep on

> **CONTEXT**
>
> Margaret Atwood remarked in 1980: 'Writing... is an act of faith; I believe it's also an act of hope, the hope that things can be better than they are.' See Margaret Atwood, *Second Words*, p. 349.

going with this sad and hungry and sordid, this limping and
mutilated story, because after all I want you to hear it, as I will
hear yours too if I ever get the chance, if I meet you or if you
escape, in the future or in Heaven or in prison or underground,
some other place. What they have in common is that they're not
here. By telling you anything at all I'm at least believing in you, I
believe you're there, I believe you into being. Because I'm telling
you this story I will your existence. I tell, therefore you are.

So I will go on. So I will myself to go on. I am coming to a part
you will not like at all, because in it I did not behave well, but I
will try nonetheless to leave nothing out. After all you've been
through, you deserve whatever I have left, which is not much but
includes the truth.

**CHECK
THE BOOK**

*Margaret Atwood:
Conversations,*
edited by Earl
Ingersoll (1992)
contains valuable
comments on
narrative techniques
in the novel.

If the preceding passages were concerned with 'writing the body',
this last one might be described as writing the story as if it were a
body. Offred begins by apologising to her readers (or listeners),
reminding us of her own compromised situation, acknowledging
the suffering and painful conditions out of which her narrative is
told. Though she remarks on her feminine attempts to lighten her
story and indirectly refers to her new love relationship with Nick,
her main emphasis is on the misery of her condition with its
boredom and its dangers. She first likens the structure of her story
to a dismembered body, but then, shifting the focus to her subject
matter, she presents her story personified as a victim of torture or
as one of the walking wounded after a battle, in imagery which not
only reminds us of daily life in Gilead but also of her storytelling
method. As a self-conscious narrator, Offred is aware of her
'limping and mutilated' narrative with its fragmented structure, its
isolated scenic units, its gaps and blanks, its dislocated time
sequence, and her own hesitations and doubts. Her story is an
eyewitness to disaster, but it is also, as she recognises, a substitute
for dialogue and an escape fantasy. As stories presuppose both
tellers and listeners, so Offred's storytelling process invents her
listeners in whom she needs to believe because she needs to gesture
towards a world outside Gilead. Her awareness of her strategy is
plain in her deliberate address to readers as '**you**' outside the text
and outside Gilead. This is emphasised by her punning variant on
Descartes's famous sentence: 'I think, therefore I am.' Offred

resists the self-enclosure of this definition of humanness, just as she rejects Descartes's insistence on the absolute separation between thought and body. She shifts the emphasis to language and communication, setting up an interaction between 'I' and 'you'. Her prison narrative is presented as the only way of bridging the gap between an isolated self and the world outside. Storytelling becomes her means of personal survival, a reconstruction of events and also a means of reconstructing her life after the traumatic disruption of her former life.

Offred's is indeed a narrative of resistance, challenging not only Gilead's perspective but also the misrepresentations of her experience in the future, for it illustrates the difference between a woman's private narrative of memory and the grand impersonal narrative of history. Having heard Offred's voice we are unlikely to accept Professor Pieixoto's scholarly gloss which consigns her, like Eurydice, to the world of the dead, or at best to the world of myth. We may not know her future but we do understand her present situation much better than the professor is willing to admit.

Perhaps the crucial point is that despite all her breaks and hesitations, Offred insists on telling her story to her unknown listeners (**'So I will myself to go on.'**) She tells it in secret and in defiance of the regime which demands total silence and submission from its Handmaids. It is her story which survives the demise of Gilead and which finally exceeds the limits that Gilead tried to impose.

? QUESTION
Discuss the relative importance of remembering and forgetting in Offred's narrative.

PART THREE

CRITICAL APPROACHES

THEMES

UTOPIAS AND DYSTOPIAS

The tradition of utopian fiction in our Western culture goes back to the Ancient Greeks with Plato's Republic, written about 350BC. Writers have always invented imaginary good societies (utopias) and imaginary bad societies (anti-utopias or **dystopias**) in order to comment on distinctive features and trends of their own societies. Utopias and anti-utopias are not merely fantasy worlds, but, as Krishan Kumar describes them in his book *Utopianism* (1991), they are imaginary places 'and accordingly futile to seek out, that nevertheless exist tantalisingly (or frighteningly) on the edge of possibility, somewhere just beyond the boundary of the real' (p. 1). These fictions always have a kind of mirror relation to the writer's own world. They may offer models for the future, or more frequently they may make **satiric** attacks on present society and deliver strong warnings against the consequences of particular kinds of political and social behaviour.

Margaret Atwood said in a review of Marge Piercy's *Woman on the Edge of Time* (1976), 'Utopias are products of the moral rather than the literary sense', and as political or social commentary they have a strongly didactic element. They need to be read with some knowledge of the context of their own time to enable the reader to see the particularities of the society in which they were produced. Sir Thomas More's *Utopia* (1516) is concerned with the possibilities for a better society that were being opened up by the discovery of the New World of America, whereas nearly 500 years later *The Handmaid's Tale* is warning against threats of environmental pollution, religious fundamentalism and state surveillance in that same New World which has become the United States of America.

Utopias and dystopias are evidently two sides of the same coin, and it is worth thinking about the **genre** or literary form to which they both belong. How do we define a genre at the present time? Today we think of genre not as a rigid classification system but

CONTEXT

The Greek philosopher Plato (c.428/7–c.348/7BC) wrote a series of dialogues, one of which is *The Republic*. In it Socrates describes the ideal state, in which the perfect forms of beauty, goodness and truth are cultivated to the exclusion of their opposites.

rather as a set of conventions or codes or 'family resemblances' (in plot or form or kind of language used) which structure the choices writers make, just as they structure our expectations as readers. These expectations are formed from all the other texts we have read, as we look for familiar signs which tell us whether to expect a detective novel or a romance, for example. **Postmodern** critics have encouraged us to see genres as social constructions, historically and ideologically responsive to the society to which they belong. Linda Hutcheon puts this position very clearly in *The Canadian Postmodern* (1988) when she emphasises how **postmodern** fiction, in which she includes *The Handmaid's Tale*, highlights specificities of location which challenge conventions that are presumed to be 'universal'. Those 'universals' can 'in fact be shown to embody the values of a very particular group of people—of a certain class, race, gender, and sexual orientation' (p. 108). Their narrative choices marginalise or neglect all other perspectives. This attitude of contestation challenges traditional systems of authority, which include literary genres as well as political systems and patriarchal structures of belief, and cultural codes. The critical emphasis is now on resistance to generic conventions, playing against them, by giving the narrative authority to people whose voices have been formerly silenced, eg. women, as Atwood does in *The Handmaid's Tale*.

Atwood is still very aware of the power of generic conventions, which form the contract between writer and reader. In an interview shortly after the publication of *The Handmaid's Tale* she commented:

> You have to understand what the [literary] form is doing, how it works, before you say, 'Now we're going to make it different, we're going to do this thing which is unusual, we're going to turn it upside down, we're going to move it so it includes something which isn't supposed to be there, we're going to surprise the reader (*Conversations*, p. 193).

She is thinking here of the dystopian genre and the crucial changes she has made to it with *The Handmaid's Tale*, for utopias and dystopias belong traditionally to a masculine genre, and she has feminised the dystopia by making her storyteller a woman. When in

CONTEXT

In classical genre theory, first spelled out by Aristotle, literary works were divided into three genres: lyric, epic and dramatic, but as new forms like the novel were invented, the concept of genre was widened to accommodate these new forms. Genre theory was always being revised and redefined according to different criteria.

1998 Atwood gave a series of talks to students in France about the writing of *The Handmaid's Tale* she spoke first of her extensive reading of utopias and dystopias, and most of her examples were written by men.

CONTEXT

Atwood began with Sir Thomas More's first venture *Utopia*, and followed this with dystopias, such as Jonathan Swift's *Gulliver's Travels* (1726), Aldous Huxley's *Brave New World* (1932), George Orwell's *Animal Farm* (1945) and *Nineteen Eighty-Four* (1949).

Atwood offers a much shorter list of utopian fictions by women that included Charlotte Perkins Gilman's *Herland* (1915) and Marge Piercy's *Woman on the Edge of Time*. She mentioned only one feminist dystopia, *The Stepford Wives*, which was made into a film in 1974 from a novel written by a man, Ira Levin. She emphasised that the meeting point between utopias and dystopias was that they were both representations of arranged societies characterised by highly regulated systems of social control and punishment for those who violated the laws of that society: 'Both utopias and dystopias have the habit of cutting off the hands and feet and even heads of those who don't fit in the scheme' (Interview in Dvorak, p. 20). Moreover, utopias could quickly change into their opposites, depending on the point of view of the narrator and whether or not he or she benefited from the new social order. As the Commander countered Offred's objections to Gilead: 'Better never means better for everyone, he says. It always means worse, for some' (p. 222).

So, the main features of a dystopia are patriarchal rule, totalitarianism, and dictatorship (as opposed to a utopian consensus of opinion on the laws, according to Atwood), social regimentation and the erasure of individual difference in the interests of a 'collective good', censorship, **propaganda**, and state control of the language used by its citizens. Here we might compare Gilead's invented biblical **rhetoric** and its new vocabulary for Handmaids' greetings and collective rituals with Orwell's Newspeak in *Nineteen Eighty-Four*, for in both cases language is changed into an instrument not for communication purposes but to smother dissenting utterances, particularly by women.

The Handmaid's Tale is an exposure of power politics at their most basic – 'Who can do what to whom' (p. 144), as Offred says. Indeed, it is women who are worst off, for in Gilead women and nature are relentlessly exploited as 'national resources'. Atwood's Gilead is her strong warning against the policies and assumptions of late twentieth-century Western technological society. As she also makes plain in the 'Historical Notes', Gilead turns out to have been an unworkable social experiment. She told an interviewer in 1987, 'I'm an optimist. I like to show that the Third Reich, the Fourth Reich, the Fifth Reich did not last forever' (*Conversations*, p. 223), and she compares her 'Historical Notes' with Orwell's note on Newspeak at the end of *Nineteen Eighty-Four*.

Many of the themes of *The Handmaid's Tale* are to be found in *Nineteen Eighty-Four*. It offers a similar warning against threats of totalitarianism in the not too distant future, and delineates the ways in which any totalitarian state tries to control not only the lives but also the thoughts of its subjects. There are similar efforts to silence opposition at any price, and both novels warn against the dangers of **propaganda** and censorship. Atwood pays particular attention to the abuses of language in Gilead where the meanings of words are changed to their opposites, as in Orwell's Newspeak, in an effort to restructure the way people are allowed to think about their world. For example, the Gileadean **rhetoric** of 'Aunts', 'Angels', 'Salvagings' takes words with reassuring emotional connotations and distorts them into **euphemisms** for the instruments of oppression.

There is, however, one major difference between *The Handmaid's Tale* and *Nineteen Eighty-Four*: Atwood's novel is told from the point of view of an 'ignorant peripherally involved woman'. (Incidentally, this is the same point of view that she adopted in her previous novel, *Bodily Harm*.)

This gender factor, which is highlighted thematically, opens up a serious debate about genre and gender, which is emphasised in the 'Historical Notes' at the end told from a masculine point of view. We need to focus our attention on the female narrator's angle to see how Atwood experiments with the dystopian genre and how a feminine perspective relates the novel to contemporary ideological and cultural issues. The shift in the narrator's gender allows us to view *The Handmaid's Tale* as a revisioning of *Nineteen Eighty-Four*. Certainly the two novels come out of different historical contexts and project different futuristic scenarios. Unlike George Orwell's book, *The Handmaid's Tale* is set in the United States and begins almost at the same point in time that Orwell's novel ended.

CHECK THE FILM

Terry Gillam's *Brazil* (1985), a futurist dystopia, offers a black comic parallel to *The Handmaid's Tale*.

UTOPIAS AND DYSTOPIAS continued

CONTEXT

Orwell's novel set in London was published in the bleak postwar period of the 1940s in the context of the Cold War, the rise of Stalinist terrorism, the building of the Berlin Wall, and pervaded by recent memories of Nazi Germany. He envisages a nightmare Europe by the early 1980s, ruled over by a totalitarian state called Oceania which is committed to terrorism and perpetual war.

Atwood deliberately leaves the time of her dystopia unspecific, though the American critic Lee Thompson cites Atwood's manuscript note which gives Offred's birth date as 1978, which would mean that her adult eye witness account of life in Gilead belongs to the first decade of the twenty-first century. Gilead has a similarly oppressive structure to Oceania, though it voices the political, social, and environmental anxieties of late twentieth-century capitalist North American culture.

Most crucially, Offred's situation and perspective are very different from Orwell's protagonist Winston Smith's. Whereas she is relegated to the political margins of Gilead and confined to domestic spaces as a conscripted Handmaid, where she is forbidden to read and write, Winston Smith reads and writes continually at the misnamed Ministry of Truth. He is employed to destroy historical records by shoving them down the 'memory hole' and to forge new historical 'facts' according to the dictates of the Party **propaganda** machine. (It would be his job to invent the kind of news reportage which Offred watches on the television in Serena Joy's sitting room.) In contrast to Winston, who lives in a nightmarish world of surveillance with giant televison screens and posters declaring 'BIG BROTHER IS WATCHING YOU' as he wanders the London streets or sits at home alone, Offred cannot see what is going on around her even when she is allowed out, because of the Handmaid's white headdress. She has only the most anecdotal knowledge of how the fundamentalist Gileadean regime came to power or how the system functions. As she says of her Commander, 'I don't know what he's a Commander of. What does he control, what is his field, as they used to say?' (p. 195). Given Offred's enforced ignorance, Atwood has to explain Gilead's political philosophy and its mechanisms of control via a male voice in the 'Historical Notes', whereas Winston understands the policies of Oceania both through his work and through the forbidden black book which he secretly reads. Indeed, Offred's narrative with its focus on the trivial events of her daily life as she looks for 'tiny peepholes' or fracture lines in the system, appears as a deliberate resistance to Orwell's masculine fascination with institutional politics and military tactics. Atwood's version focuses on those very things which Orwell left out of his dystopia, so that her story shifts the structural relations between the private and public worlds to which Orwell, like his male predecessors, conformed. Instead, Offred's story concentrates on the concerns of the officially silenced others. The endings are different too, for Atwood's novel opens the ambiguous possibility for Offred's escape, whereas there is no escape for Winston Smith or for his lover Julia, who are broken by the system. Winston is brainwashed into loving Big Brother by the end, whereas Offred never comes to love the Commander. Instead, with the help of her lover Nick she manages to escape for at least as long as it takes her to tell her story of feminine resistance and provisional survival.

Certainly Atwood's purpose is political, though her agenda is far broader than Orwell's as it takes in sexual power politics, state power politics, and Canadian-American relations. It also engages with global issues relating to the environment and historical components that range from European colonialism to events closer to the 1980s relating to what Atwood saw on her travels in Iran and Afghanistan, and to newspaper reports on Ceaucescu's Romania and the rise of the religious Right in America.

The novel is set in the United States, because, as Atwood has said, 'The States are more extreme in everything … Everyone watches the States to see what the country is doing and might be doing ten or fifteen years from now' (*Conversations*, p. 217). Her comment reflects not only American economic and cultural imperialism but also the continuing American dominance over the Canadian imagination. 'Watching Big Brother' could be the subtitle for Atwood's book. This is a futuristic scenario but close enough to our time, for the protagonist herself has grown up in the permissive society of the 1970s and 1980s and is at the time of telling her story only thirty-three years old. Some of the features of Gilead could apply to any late twentieth-century state with advanced technology and pollution problems. It is, however, specifically an American location, as we learn not only from the 'Historical Notes', but also from details within Offred's narrative, as, for example, from the Gileadean takeover 'when they shot the President and machine-gunned the Congress' (p. 183), Moira's escape along Mass Avenue (p. 257), and 4 July, the former Independence Day (p. 209). Atwood signals the particular historical, social and political context in her 'What if' statement (see **Reading *The Handmaid's Tale***). There is also a strong sense of American Puritan history here, establishing connections

CHECK THE NET
For further information on the New Right in America, a reliable starting point for your search would be: **http://www. publiceye.org/ research/policy.html.**

between seventeenth-century New England's witch hunts and late twentieth-century Gilead, with its New Right ideology and its religious fanaticism (See **Historical and political context**).

Not only is it a 'Back to the Future' scenario but it is also a period of crisis, for the novel deals with the new anti-utopian society at its moment of transition. Offred herself is facing both ways, but so is Gilead, with all its citizens and its leaders remembering the capitalist era and its culture. Gilead is a bizarre mixture of fundamentalist principles, late twentieth-century technology and a Hollywood-style **propaganda** machine. It also has the whole of human history upon which to draw, for 'there was little that was truly original with or indigenous to Gilead: its genius was synthesis' ('Historical Notes', p. 319). The novel ends as a strong warning to learn from history in order to avoid a nightmare like Gilead for our own future.

It is a reminder that this novel exists on that borderline territory between history and prophecy which is one of the dominant characteristics of the dystopian genre.

Offred's tale shifts the emphasis of the dystopia from the masculine centre to the marginalised feminine perspective. Her main interest is not on 'political' in the sense of state power politics or even Ofglen's Mayday resistance movement. Instead her narrative is a version of the 1970s feminist slogan, 'The Personal is Political', for her 'little narrative ' challenges the absolute authority of Gilead's heroic 'grand narrative' of history by chronicling an alternative feminised version. I shall end this section by reminding you of what Atwood said about writers in her 1981 Amnesty International address, when she was already thinking about *The Handmaid's Tale*: 'The writer retains three attributes that power-mad regimes cannot tolerate: a human imagination, in the many forms it may take; the power to communicate; and hope' (*Second Words*, p. 397). That comment could of course be made about Atwood as woman novelist and about Offred as female storyteller.

FEMINISM

The Handmaid's Tale provides a brief history and critique of the North American feminist movement since the 1960s, for as Offred reminds us, 'Context is all' (p. 202).

? QUESTION
How does *The Handmaid's Tale* work to shock readers into a recognition of the evils of our contemporary world?

With her deep distrust of ideological hardlines, Atwood refuses to simplify the gender debate or to swallow slogans whole. Instead, she shows how slogans always run the risk of being taken over as instruments of oppression, like the 1970s' feminist catchphrases 'a women's culture' or 'The Personal is Political', which Gilead has appropriated. The novel is firmly situated in its historical and geographical context of America in the 1980s with its liberal anxieties over both women's rights and civil rights. These had been threatened by the rise of the American neo-conservative movement in the late 1970s which attained its maximum political force under Ronald Reagan's presidency after 1980.

Offred's memory narrative represents important documentary evidence of cultural history which includes the rise of second wave feminism and the antifeminist backlash of New Right Christian fundamentalism. All the women in the novel are survivors of 'the time before' and their voices represent a range of traditional feminine and new feminist positions dating back to the Women's Liberation movement of the late 1960s. Offred's mother, a single parent, belongs to this early activist group with its campaigns for women's sexual freedom, its pro-abortion rallies and pornographic book burnings.

While De Beauvoir showed women that their inferior status was not due to their biological weakness but to historical and economic assumptions about femaleness, Friedan and Greer placed much more emphasis on women's bodies and issues relating to female sexuality. Their focus was on issues around motherhood, abortion, and reproductive technologies, pornography and violence against women, women's right to equal pay, as well as extending into environmentalism and peace campaigns. The feminist movement rapidly gained strength in the United States, winning Congressional endorsement of the Equal Rights Amendment in 1972 and the Supreme Court decision to make abortion legal in 1973. However, opposition campaigns and lobbying by the New Right and pro-life campaigners meant that the Equal Rights Amendment (ERA) failed to be ratified in 1982, a bitter defeat for feminism at that time. Offred also comments ruefully on her own indifference to her mother's feminist activism and laments the political apathy of so many younger women which contributed to

> **CONTEXT**
>
> As Atwood remarked in 1982, '*Feminist* is now one of the all-purpose words. It really can mean anything from people who think men should be pushed off cliffs to people who think it's O.K. for women to read and write. All those could be called feminist positions. Thinking that it's O.K. for women to read and write would be a radically feminist position in Afghanistan. So what do you mean?' (*Conversations*, p. 140).

> **CONTEXT**
>
> The heroines of this era were Simone de Beauvoir (*The Second Sex*, translated into English in 1952), Betty Friedan (*The Feminine Mystique*, 1963) and Germaine Greer (*The Female Eunuch*, 1970).

FEMINISM continued

CHECK THE BOOK

For a useful history of Anglo-American feminism, see *Feminisms: A Reader* (1992), edited by Maggie Humm.

CHECK THE BOOK

Read what Margaret Atwood has to say about feminism in her book *Conversations*: 'As for Woman, capital W, we got stuck with that for centuries. Eternal woman. But really, "Woman" is the sum total of women. It doesn't exist apart from that, except as an abstracted idea' (p. 201).

the rise to power of extreme right wing. As she now realises, 'We lived as usual, by ignoring. Ignoring isn't the same as ignorance, you have to work at it' (p. 66).

The opponents to feminism are represented in the novel by the Commander's Wife and the Aunts, who show they are more than willing to collaborate with Gilead's regime to re-educate women back into traditional gender roles. Among the Handmaids, younger women who grew up in the 1970s and 1980s, positions are equally varied, from those who accept the female victim role (like Janine), to radicals like the lesbian feminist Moira, to Offred herself, whose story highlights the **paradoxes** and dilemmas within contemporary feminism. As Gilead is quick to point out, women's sexual and economic freedom of choice have brought new anxieties, though their grotesque distortion of the dangerous consequences of feminism discredit their critiques.

Just as there are many different kinds of women, so there is no simple division between masculine and feminine qualities: if men are capable of violence, then so are women – think of Aunt Lydia or the Particicution. *The Handmaid's Tale* may be a critique of certain feminist positions though it is clear where its sympathies lie, and Offred's double vision allows her to evaluate both Gilead and her own lost late twentieth-century America: that was not entirely good, but Gilead is undoubtedly worse. Atwood insists that women have never marched under a single banner.

Indeed, how could feminism be anything but plural when issues of class, race and sexuality are as important as gender in shaping anyone's identity? It is Offred, the witty, sceptical woman who cares about men, about mother-daughter relationships and about her female friends, who survives to tell her story. Some critics have seen this novel as a feminist **dystopia**, but as the narrative demonstrates, it is a failed utopia for everyone. Everything is in short supply, from rationing of foodstuffs and goods, to the lack of sexual choice for both women and men. With the sharp decline in the birthrate and reproduction assuming primary importance, women are reduced to their biological function as childbearers and denied any sexual freedom at all at any age, but that national crisis has affected men's lifestyles as well. Any male practice which inhibits reproduction is severely punished, so that male doctors who formerly practised abortion, or homosexuals, or Roman Catholic priests (as well as nuns) who took vows of chastity are all executed and their bodies hung on the Wall. Pornography, sexual violence and infidelity are all outlawed, but so is falling in love. *The Handmaid's Tale* challenges state tyranny and social engineering which rules out any dimension of choice, emotion, or free will for women as well as for most men. The novel should be seen as being more comprehensive than just a feminist dystopia for its concerns extend to include gender politics and basic human rights.

NARRATIVE TECHNIQUES

The Handmaid's Tale is a woman's autobiographical narrative that challenges the absolute authority of Gilead, highlighting the significance of storytelling as an act of resistance against oppression, thereby making a particular kind of individual political statement. We might approach Offred's narrative through Atwood's own comments as a writer who is also an active member of Amnesty International:

> I'm an artist ... and in any monolithic regime I would be shot. They always do that to artists. Why? Because the artists are messy. They don't fit. They make squawking noises. They protest. They insist on some kind of standard of humanity which any such regime is going to violate. They will violate it saying that it's for the good of all, or the good of the many, or the better this or better that. And the artists will always protest and they'll always get shot. Or go into exile. (*Conversations*, p. 183)

This statement on the writer's role provides a gloss on Offred's position as teller of this tale, for she insists on voicing her own point of view when the regime demands total silence. But Offred's freedom is very circumscribed and she cannot tell her story within the Gileadean context. She can only tell it after she has escaped. We learn at the end that what we have read is a transcript of a jumble of cassette recordings that have been found on an archaeological site. What we have is a later reconstruction of Offred's reconstruction told after her escape, and by the time of our reading Offred herself has disappeared. Yet storytelling is the only possible gesture against the silences of death and of history.

? QUESTION Offred describes her narrative as 'This limping and mutilated story'. How does this image relate to either the content or the structure of *The Handmaid's Tale*?

CHECK THE BOOK

Two of Atwood's other novels are women's prison narratives. See *Bodily Harm* (1981) and *Alias Grace* (1996).

In an analysis of narrative techniques we might begin by describing her story as a woman's prison narrative. Just as Offred herself was enclosesd by her Handmaid's costume and entrapped in the domestic spaces of the Commander's house, so her story is enclosed by the prefatory quotations and the 'Historical Notes' at the end. It is framed by references to patriarchal power across history, with the references to Mary Webster (Atwood's own ancestor) who was hanged as a witch in seventeenth century New England, to Swift's eighteenth-century pamphlet, *A Modest Proposal,* which **satirically** recommends that Irish women be treated as 'national resources' for breeding children, to the Old Testament story of Jacob's Handmaid. (Only the Sufi proverb eludes this classification.) The 'Historical Notes' project this oppression far into the future, as we learn that Offred's story as we have it has been transcribed by male historians who seem intent on devaluing if not discrediting her tale. Yet Offred's voice survives even if it comes to us in a provisional form `based on some guesswork' (p. 314), and her narrative shows how she resists the tyranny of Gilead with its deterministic view of history.

Offred is like Mary Webster who did not die despite being hanged, and Atwood has told that story as another autobiographical fiction in her poetic sequence 'Half-Hanged Mary' where Mary's assertion of being alive echoes Offred's: '*I hurt, therefore I am*' (*Eating Fire: Selected Poetry*, p. 327). Mary survived fourteen years after her hanging, realising that history is made of accidents and so it is the opposite of deterministic. Just as she experienced and survived the arbitrariness of Puritan laws, so Offred sees and resists the arbitrariness of Gilead's rules. Like Mary, Offred is 'determined to last' so that her story might more appropriately be seen as a woman's survival narrative rather than a prison narrative. Indeed, one of her major survival strategies is her secret storytelling, for she is the voice of the excluded other within the heartland of Gilead. Her narrative is a discontinuous one, with its frequent time shifts, short scenes, and its unfinished ending. As Margaret Atwood has said, '[Offred] was boxed in. How do you tell a narrative from the point of view of that person? The more limited and boxed in you are, the more important details become ... Details, episodes separate themselves from the flow of time in which they're embedded.' (*Conversations*, p. 216).

CHECK THE BOOK

For Atwood's comments on the rise of the religious Right in America, see Nathalie Cooke, *Margaret Atwood: A Biography* (1998), Chapter 19.

One of the first things we notice is the way the story shifts abruptly from one scene to another and from present time to the past, so that the narrator's present situation and her past history are only gradually revealed. Reading is an exercise of reconstruction as we piece together present details with fragments of remembered experience, revealed by **flashbacks**. At the beginning there are few flashbacks, for we, like the narrator, are trapped in present time. The first flashback occurs in Chapter 3 and there are brief references to Luke in Chapters 2 and 5. However, it is in the 'Night' sections that the flashback technique is most obvious and most sustained, for this is Offred's 'time out' when she is free to wander back into her remembered past. It is here that we gain a sense of Offred as a powerful personal presence with a history.

It is a good idea when reading the novel to make a brief summary of every chapter, for this will enable you to see how inner psychological details and particulars of the external world are recorded. You will also be able to use this evidence to trace the mosaic method used in structuring the novel out of scenic units.

To return to the topic of how Offred's storytelling and her survival are linked, it is worth noting that the theme of survival – for an individual, for a nation, and collectively for the human species – has always been one of Atwood's central preoccupations. Back in 1972 she wrote a book called *Survival: A Thematic Guide to Canadian Literature*, where she outlined several meanings of the word 'survival', though the main meaning was 'staying alive', where 'the survivor has little after this ordeal that he did not have before, except gratitude for having escaped with his life' (*Survival*, p. 33) – or *her* life, in the case of Offred or Mary Webster. Offred's first priority is to survive physically in the dangerous political climate of Gilead, where everyone is under constant surveillance at home or on the streets, and death is an everyday possibility. A Handmaid is particularly vulnerable if she fails to produce a baby for the state after being 'posted' to three different Commanders. (As Offred ironically remarks of her own childless situation in this her final posting: *'Give me children or else I die'* (p. 71) has only one unambiguous meaning in Gilead for somebody like her.) She is determined to survive, as we know from the beginning when she arrives at the Commander's house: 'I am alive, I live, I breathe, I put

CONTEXT

In *Survival* Atwood was already exploring Canadian-American relations, where she emphasised the identity of Canada as separate from the United States, Britain and France, focused through Canada's favourite cultural myths of the wilderness.

my hand out, unfolded, into the sunlight' (p. 18). She retains this vigorous survival instinct even in the most threatening circumstances, and in fact she is shocked to find her body still almost independently asserting its demands even after the horrible Particicution ceremony. Sickened by what she has witnessed, she still wants to eat: 'Maybe it's because I've been emptied; or maybe it's the body's way of seeing to it that I remain alive, continue to report its bedrock prayer: *I am, I am.* I am, still' (p. 293). Only near the end does she almost succumb to despair, though even then she does does not wish to die but to 'keep on living, in any form', however abjectly (p. 298).

Offred's second priority is how to survive psychologically and emotionally after the trauma of separation from her husband and child and her period of indoctrination at the Rachel and Leah Centre, and this is where survival strategies and narrative techniques come together in the choices Offred makes. In her determination to resist Gilead's efforts to erase her individual identity and in order to retain her sanity she tells herself stories, reminding herself of who she was in 'the time before', recognising where she is now, and hoping against hope for the future. Her storytelling is deliberately balanced between her narrative of memory and her record of the present centred on her physical environment, which is both her external surroundings and more intimately her own bodily experiences.

> **? QUESTION**
> Why is the account of 'Birth Day' (Section 7) positioned at the centre of the novel?

Offred sees her body as a place, like her room, which she inhabits in spatial terms; she calls it 'my own territory ... where only I know the footing' (p. 83). The story of her female body with its biological rhythms and its potential to produce children is the only part of her narrative in which Gilead is interested. **Ironically**, it is her body rather than her wishes or her will which is at the centre of household arrangements: 'Even the Commander is subject to its whims' (p. 91). She resists Gilead's essentialist definitions of herself by telling not only the story of her physiology but also her sensations, emotions and desires, showing that she has the power to tell a different story from the one already scripted for her. We might look at where she talks about her body as a wilderness, or her womb as dark cosmic space with the moon gliding across it every month, or at her volcanic laughter which wells up from inside her body like a stream of blood from a broken artery (See **Language** and **Imagery**, also **Detailed commentaries, Text 2**). Everything about Offred's body and her desires exceeds the authority of Gilead, most crucially in her love story with Nick, where he pays attention 'only to the possiblities of my body' (p. 282). It is through this transgressive love affair that Offred's story of emotional survival is told most fully, for it is with Nick that she rediscovers 'the marvellous text of herself' (to quote Hélène Cixous in 'The Laugh of the Medusa'). Their romance challenges the limits of Gilead's power to control the life stories of its citizens, for 'falling in love' was precisely one of the activities that the regime had edited out.

However, this close-up body focus represents another form of imprisonment in the time trap of the present, where Offred feels she is living with her face pressed up against a wall. Only in memory and imagination does she have any freedom of choice, and it is through storytelling that she can invent a multidimensional life for herself: 'What I need is perspective. The illusion of depth ... Otherwise you live in the moment. Which is not where I want to be' (p. 153). Most of her stories are memory narratives triggered off by association with places or events in the present. As she says, 'You'll have to forgive me. I'm a refugee from the past, and like other refugees I go over the customs and habits of being I've left or been forced to leave behind me' (p. 239). The narrative represents the complex ways that memory works, where the present moment is never self-contained but pervaded by traces of other times and events. Frequently there is an overlap, for she is always beset by double vision, seeing the present through her memories of the past, living in a familiar place which has become defamiliarised by the revolution. Everywhere she walks in this, her home town of Cambridge, Massachusetts, leads her straight into the landscape of memory: 'To the right, if you could walk along, there's a street that would take you down towards the river. There's a boathouse where they kept the sculls once, and some bridges' (p. 40). As she looks at the shops with their outlandish pictorial signs, she remembers what they used to be before their names were changed, like Lilies of the Field, which used to be a cinema that had its annual Humphrey Bogart festival.

 **CHECK THE BOOK**
For a detailed account of autobiography in the feminine, see the essay by Sherrill Grace, 'Gender as Genre: Atwood's Autobiographical "I"', in Colin Nicholson, ed. *Margaret Atwood: Writing and Subjectivity*, 1994.

However, memory is more than a breath of nostalgia for Offred. It is her chief escape mechanism, representing 'somewhere good' as space and time are collapsed into each other: 'The night is my time out. Where should I go?' (p. 47) She selects from her memorybank which story she will tell about absent presences, like her dearest friend Moira, her mother, her little daughter, her husband Luke. So, while these may be stories of loss and mourning, they are also imaginative resurrections, for she says when remembering Moira, 'I've tried to make it sound as much like her as I can. It's a way of keeping her alive' (p. 256). In an odd way the plot endorses Offred's efforts by staging the reappearances of all these female figures. Moira is there in Gilead in the flesh twice, while Offred's mother's ghost is resurrected twice (on films which Moira tells Offred she sees at the Rachel and Leah Centre in Chapters 7 and 39), and Offred's daughter is brought back in a photograph which Serena Joy shows to her (Chapter 35). Of course these presences do not remain with Offred, so that her story is very ambivalent with bursts of joy balanced by stabs of pain at their loss and her recognition of her own powerlessness. Her storytelling cannot change the social fabric of Gilead though it does grant her the power to imagine differently and so her storytelling becomes an act of psychological survival.

Offred is not fixed in the past; indeed she is also, like Pamela (in Samuel Richardson's epistolary novel *Pamela* of 1742), writing about the present, and her record of daily life is presented with scrupulous attention to realistic detail. She records the unexciting monotony of her daily life as a Handmaid, as well as its crises, both public and personal. There are the public meetings like the Birth Day, the Prayvaganza and the terrible Salvaging; there is of course the monthly Ceremony as a semi-public event; there are her own significant private events, like her secret meetings with the Commander and their outing to Jezebel's. However ambivalent her feelings for the Commander may be, Offred recognises that it is through these meetings in his study where she can talk and read that she is enabled to return to a lively sense of herself as an individual. Most crucial for her is her love affair with Nick (Chapters 40 and 41), which has all the conventional features of a romantic love story and possibly even a happy ending. Yet in the circumstances it is the most unlikely plot that could have been devised, and Offred tells it with a kind of dazzled disbelief in its reality.

CHECK THE BOOK

In *Pamela* by Samuel Richardson (1689–1761), the heroine left penniless at the age of fifteen is pursued by her dead employer's son, who in turn imprisons her, offers to make her his mistress, and attempts to rape her. But virtue prevails. Eventually she marries him and becomes a model wife. The story is told in the form of letters from six different people.

Offred tells the stories of many other women as well as her own. Some of these are fixed in the past and some end even while she is telling her own. Moira's story, like her mother's, is one of female heroism but, unlike her mother's, Moira's story extends into the present, for she too becomes an inmate at the Rachel and Leah Centre, and Offred recalls with delight Moira's courage and outrageousness in Chapters 13, 15 and 22. Offred finds Moira again at Jezebel's in Chapter 37 and tells the story of her life as a rebel in Chapter 38. Hers is one of the unfinished stories embedded in this narrative, for Offred never sees Moira again after that night.

There are also shorter story fragments about other Handmaids, all of them rebels or victims or both, which form a sad subtext to Offred's survival narrative and incidentally imply a moral judgment on the social engineering policies of Gilead. There is the story of her unnamed predecessor at the Commander's house, of whom all she knows is the scribbled secret message (Chapter 9) and scraps of information about how she hanged herself (Chapter 29). For Offred, that woman is her own ghostly double: 'How could I have believed I was alone in here? There were always two of us. Get it over, she says' (p. 305).

The motif of doubles recurs in the story of Ofglen: 'Doubled, I walk the street' (p. 33). Yet Ofglen turns out to be more like Moira's double than Offred's, for she too is a rebel in disguise, a member of the Mayday Resistance movement and a whisperer of irreverent comments at the Prayvaganza. But her story does have an ending, for she commits suicide after the Salvaging (Chapter 44).

Whether women are rebels or willing victims, their chances of survival are slim, as the story of Janine illustrates. She appears and reappears, marking the various stages of a Handmaid's career – from willing victim at the Rachel and Leah Centre where she almost has a nervous breakdown (Chapter 33), to her moment of triumph as the pregnant Ofwarren whose Birth Day is attended by all the Handmaids (Chapters 19 and 21), to her last frightening appearance as madwoman after the Particicution, holding a clump of bloodstained hair (Chapter 43). She too is one of Offred's doubles, a dreadful warning of what could happen if she gave up hope.

? QUESTION
In what ways are Offred's mother, Moira, and the Commander important to her life in Gilead?

? QUESTION
After watching the film version of the novel, compare and contrast the novel and the film, investigating the reasons for their differences.

Offred also tells the story of the Commander's Wife, with **flashbacks** to her earlier career as a television personality on a gospel show in Chapters 3 and 8. In a curious way, though it could not be seen as an example of female bonding, Offred's account presents Serena Joy as another of her own doubles, trapped like herself by Gileadean ideology. In one of her odder anecdotes, Offred is even disguised as Serena Joy when she has to wear her blue cloak to go with the Commander to Jezebel's, and she is forced to look at her own face in Serena Joy's silver mirror to put on her make-up.

Offred insists on telling the stories of other silenced women which contradict Gilead's claims to absolute mastery and its myth of female submissiveness. From a wide historical perspective, she can be seen as writing against the Old Testament dismissal of the Handmaids of the Patriarchs, and she is writing on behalf of all those women then and now with no rights of representation. In this way her narrative is exemplary and **symbolic**. (It could even be compared with those eighteenth-century American slave narratives which Margaret Atwood recalls in her oblique reference to the 'Underground Railroad' for slaves escaping from the United States to Canada.)

There is yet another dimension to Offred's complex narrative, which signals the **postmodern** contemporary nature of Margaret Atwood's storytelling technique. Offred is continually drawing our attention to her storytelling process, commenting on the way that the act of telling shapes and changes real experience, and giving reasons why she needs to tell her story at all (see Chapters 7, 23, 40 and 41).

Sometimes addressing the reader as 'Dear You' (p. 49, for example), she deliberately draws the reader into the action as it happens, guiding us in our role as participants and engaging us in her moral dilemmas. Offred sounds remarkably like Atwood herself who remarked in 1980 that 'the process of reading is part of the process of writing, the necessary completion without which writing can hardly be said to exist' (*Second Words*, p. 345). Offred is a self conscious narrator who recognises that texts are created by their readers as well as by their writers , so that meanings are not fixed by the narrator but may have different resonances for different readers

QUESTION
Discuss the role of the reader 'Dear You' as an implied presence in the novel.

in the light of their own experiences. Her recognition that she does not have ultimate authority over what her story means and that meanings are always a matter of perspective is one of the markers of postmodernism in this novel. Indeed, Offred is always questioning herself on how 'true' her story is, or where the boundaries lie between fiction and reality. Is it a story she is telling? As she comments, 'Tell, rather than write, because I have nothing to write with and writing is in any case forbidden' (p. 49).

That is a salutary reminder that although we are reading Offred's narrative in written form, it is actually a woman's oral narrative , and this is confirmed at the end in the professor's conference presentation. Offred also draws our attention to the fact that her telling is reconstruction after events have happened, and that she is not always a trustworthy narrator. When she is telling us about her first sexual encounter with Nick in Chapter 40, she teases us by giving us several versions, at the end of which she says, 'It didn't happen that way either. I'm not sure how it happened, not exactly' (p. 275). After all, memory like language is not entirely reliable when it comes to reconstructing reality. For Offred storytelling serves many functions: as her main survival technique, it allows her both to record her present circumstances in an eye-witness account, but it also allows her to escape from the present back into memory or forward into the future, always hoping for the day when she will get out of Gilead and be reunited with Luke and her lost daughter. It is also a substitute for dialogue as the storyteller invents her listeners: 'By telling you anything at all, I'm at least believing in you, I believe you're there, I believe you into existence' (p. 279). Offred also knows it is the only message she can send to the outside world from her imprisonment and she struggles to tell it, trusting that one day her message will be delivered: 'A story is like a letter. *Dear You*, I'll say. Just *you*, without a name... *You can mean thousands*' (p. 50). Like the Ancient Mariner, Offred's compulsion to tell compels us to listen: 'After all you've been through, you deserve whatever I have left, which is not much but includes the truth' (p. 280).

Offred's own story ends when she climbs up into the black truck, but the novel does not end here. There is a supplement in the 'Historical Notes', told by a different narrator, in a different place,

> **CONTEXT**
>
> In Samuel Taylor Coleridge's *Rime of the Ancient Mariner*, the narrator who alone of all his crew survives horrendous experiences at sea, lives on and is condemned as a penance to 'pass from land to land' retelling his tale with his 'strange power of speech'.

at a different time, projecting a second vision of the future set not in America but in Canada. (Atwood never forgets that she is a Canadian, and from one perspective this novel might be read as an example of Canadian-American dialogue.) **Paradoxically**, this shift works to convince us of the immediacy of Offred's narrative. It is very likely that we will reject the professor's dismissal of Offred as a figure belonging to the vanished past, and given his own sexist attitudes, we might assume that Offred's story about patriarchal attitudes does not belong exclusively to the past but threatens the future as well. Offred's message has been delivered 200 years later. So it is given over to us, the readers, and we are left to puzzle out the answers to all the questions she has raised.

HISTORICAL NOTES

The 'Historical Notes' are not part of Offred's narrative, but they are part of the novel and they function as a necessary supplement to her story, helping us to put one woman's autobiographical record into historical perspective. Told by a male narrator, Professor Pieixoto from the University of Cambridge, England, at an academic conference 200 years after Offred tells her story, these 'Notes' introduce another futuristic scenario which is different from the story of Gilead.

> **QUESTION**
> How do the Historical Notes alter your perspective on the novel?

At the University of Denay, Nunavit, up in Arctic Canada, women and Native peoples obviously have some status, for the Chair is a woman professor, Maryann Crescent Moon, and the conference participants go on nature walks and eat fish from the sea (Arctic Char), which suggests an unpolluted environment very different from Gilead. However, Professor Pieixoto's jokes about '*tail*' and 'Frailroads' (p. 313) suggest that the old sexist attitudes have not changed very much in 200 years. In this context Pieixoto's name is very significant. Atwood got the name (which is Portuguese) from a Brazilian novel where Pieixoto was the name of a character who keeps being reincarnated in the same form, century after century. He exemplifies the same masculinist values as the Gilead regime who had modelled themselves as the Sons of Jacob on Old Testament patriarchs. His masculinist view leads him to reconstruct the social theory of Gilead and to compare its system with many other examples of tyranny: 'As I have said elsewhere, there was little that was truly original with or indigenous to Gilead: its genius was synthesis' (p. 319). He establishes a historical context for Offred's narrative, just as he gives a detailed account of how her story was recovered from old cassette tapes made between the 1960s and the 1980s, but for all his mass of social data, he is not concerned with Offred as an individual. He is interested in establishing the authenticity of her tale and its value as objective historical evidence, while sidestepping the critical moral issues raised by her account: 'Our job is not to censure but to understand' (p. 315). He does not seem to be as interested in finding out her identity as he is in establishing the identity of her Commander. He offers two possible identifications: Waterford, who 'possessed a background in market research', (p. 319) or the more sinister figure of Judd, who was involved with the CIA. Offred has already told us that her Commander was in 'market research' (p. 195), but Professor Pieixoto does not seem to regard her testimony as reliable. His reconstruction makes a radical shift from 'herstory' to 'history' as he tries to discredit Offred's narrative by accusing her of not paying attention to important things. He does not take notice of what she has chosen to tell, a tale of the suffering and oppression of all women and most men in Gilead. As a result, the reader may feel that it is the professor who is paying attention to the wrong things. His account obliterates Offred as a person; he never tells what happened to her because he does not know and apparently is not interested. **Ironically**, he does exactly what Offred predicted would happen to the story of the Handmaids: 'From the point of view of future history, we'll be invisible' (p. 240). He is abusing Offred as Gilead abused her, removing her authority over her own life story and renaming it in a gesture similar to Gilead's suppression of a woman's identity in the Handmaid's role. The change in voice from Offred's personal, subjective account to Professor Pieixoto's generalised academic discourse forces us to take up a moral position on what we have just read, to become engaged readers. The novel ends on a question which invites us to enter the debate, having heard two opposite perspectives on the story. This is the point at which Atwood's novel assumes the didactic tone which is a distinctive mark of anti-utopian (dystopian) fiction, as it moves beyond the confines of an imagined world to become a warning to us of a future to be avoided in real life.

> **CONTEXT**
>
> Atwood's novel has been described as 'a cultural reference point' because of its factual bases. As she stated in 2001: 'In *The Handmaid's Tale* I was very careful to have nothing that we hadn't already done, or for which we didn't already have the technology, we could do it all, we have done it all.'

LANGUAGE AND IMAGERY

The allusions to Western cultural history in *The Handmaid's Tale* are extremely wide-ranging, stretching from the Bible to late twentieth-century feminism and environmental issues. There are also references to seventeenth-century American Puritanism, the slave trade, Nazism and pornographic films, as well as motifs from fairytales, quotations from Shakespeare, John Milton, René Descartes, Alfred, Lord Tennyson, Sigmund Freud and Karl Marx. The 'Historical Notes' add another layer of reference in an effort to set Gilead within an international history of totalitarianism and various forms of institutional oppression. This formidable range of references is part of Margaret Atwood's strategy for constructing her modern anti-utopia, and it is also a mark of her own high level of cultural literacy. But the novel is not at all daunting, for it uses allusions very wittily, one of its functions being to mesh together social details with which we are all familiar in order to show us how they might be shaped into a pattern for a future which we would choose to avoid.

It is Offred's narrative voice transcribed into text which situates her as an individual woman grounded in place and time, whose identity transcends that of her Handmaid's role. Through the language she uses, rather than the events of the story she tells, Offred convinces us of her resistance to Gilead's values. Her relation to language is highlighted, for language plays an important role in any discourse of power and in determining anybody's perceptions of reality. Offred's outer life is very constricted and drained of emotion, but her inner life has an energy and lyricism which enable her to survive emotionally as well as physically in the stony soil of Gilead. There is a marked difference between the language she uses to record her muted everyday life, and the language of her real life of feeling and memory, which is expressed through a richly worked vocabulary of images. These register her entirely different perception of herself and her world from the one imposed by Gilead. In her Handmaid's role Offred's language of description – of her room, the household, her walks, and the Ceremony – emphasises her isolation. She deliberately filters out emotion for as long as possible, though it seeps in through her imagery. One example of this would be when she likens the blank space on the ceiling where the light fitting has

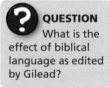

CHECK THE BOOK

For a discussion of Offred's narrative voice, see M. Dvorak, 'What's in a Name? Readers as both Pawns and Partners of Margaret Atwood's Strategy of Control', in J-M. Lacroix and J. Leclaire, eds, *Margaret Atwood: The Handmaid's Tale / Le Conte de la servante,* 1998.

QUESTION

What is the effect of biblical language as edited by Gilead?

been removed to a 'wreath' or a 'frozen halo' (p. 17). Behind the blankness lies Offred's insistent fears of torture, injury and death. Sometimes her realistic recording is overlaid by memories of the past closely associated with particular places that she passes on her walks, so that the present dissolves into landscapes of memory. Often however, she defends herself against nostalgia by playing with language, endlessly exploring the potential for multiple meanings in a word. She has a great love for puns as she delights in the arbitrary connections between words which sound the same but have different meanings. An example would be when sitting in a chair alone in her room she thinks about the word 'chair' and how it may refer to 'the leader of a meeting' or 'a mode of execution' (p. 120). Working across language borders, she thinks how the same word has an entirely different meaning in French, where it is the word for 'flesh' (p. 120). Such word play is evidence of Offred's sharpness of mind as well as her moral refusal to flatten out language as Gilead does, which only leads to confusion. It is a kind of amusement for her, while it also sensitises readers to the value of words, warning us to avoid the linguistic traps that political **rhetoric** specialises in.

CHECK THE BOOK
For further analysis of 'writing the female body' see C. A. Howells, *Margaret Atwood*, 1996, pp. 137–9.

Another of Offred's everyday strategies for mental survival is her use of **irony**, in her lively awareness of the gaps between appearance and reality, as well as her sense of the absurd. It would be wrong to forget the comic dimension in this novel, for her simmering humour bubbles up, as we have seen, even in the Ceremony – 'There's something hilarious about this' (p. 106) – and when she is invited by the Commander to play an illicit game of Scrabble with him it is all she can do not to 'shriek with laughter, fall off my chair' (p. 148). Indeed, she marks this crucial turning point in their relationship by her muffled explosion of laughter as soon as she gets back to her room. Her language at this point displays a disturbing mixture of merriment and hysteria tinged with irony. She likens her laughter to an epileptic fit which comes upon her involuntarily, and the images she uses are not simply about loss of control but quite specifically about splitting, breakage and damage, to the point where she explodes: 'Red all over the cupboard, mirth rhymes with birth' (p. 156). Standing in the cupboard, she is aware of her predecessor's message, and her laughter is tinged with an ironic awareness that she, like the other hanged Handmaid, is trapped: 'There's no way out of here' (p. 156). However, her slightly changed circumstances give Offred cause for hope, which is cautiously signalled in her last word of this episode – not 'open' (not yet) but 'opening' (p. 156).

Of course that Scrabble game appeals to Offred because it gives her a new opportunity to play with language, to resurrect obscure words like 'zygote' and even to make up nonsense words. Her delight is almost physical as she likens the letters in the game to candies: 'I would like to put them into my mouth ... the letter C. Crisp, slightly acid on the tongue, delicious' (p. 149). Critics have suggested that the words Offred uses in the game may encode her private subtext of protest against the regime with its sexual coercion and its silencing of women, with 'larynx' ,'valance', and 'zygote', followed later by 'quandary' and 'rhythm'. That may be so, though the protest is very oblique, for these words are scattered among others which could not possibly have that significance, and together they make up a list of the most valuable words for gaining points in a Scrabble game. It is no wonder that Offred often wins, though out of good manners she sometimes lets the Commander win a game.

However, these word games are only 'tiny peepholes' (p. 31) in the surface dimensions of Offred's everyday life, as she adapts Gilead's patriarchal script in ways that are by turn sceptical, defiant, or determinedly hopeful. At least this allows her to survive psychologically, although her private narrative which is the secret of her emotional survival is focused on memory and her own female body. It is her discourse of the body, chronicling her physical sensations, emotions and desires, which provides the lyrical dimension of this novel in her use of poetic imagery and imaginary landscapes. In writing about her body Offred shows how a feminine voice can find a way of speaking even when silenced by the dominant male order. Her intimate narrative is as subversive as the flowers in the Commander's Wife's garden: 'Whatever is silenced will clamour to be heard, though silently' (p. 161).

You will have noticed that there are a small number of recurrent images which form patterns or 'image clusters' throughout her narrative. They derive from the human body (hands, feet, faces, eyes, blood, wombs), also from non-human nature (flowers, gardens, changing seasons, colour and light – especially moonlight).

CHECK THE FILM
Bryan Forbes's *The Stepford Wives* (1974) is a contemporary American feminist dystopia, where suburban housewives are replaced by robotic models.

(See **Detailed commentaries, Texts 1 and 2**). Offred's images, all related to nature and organic processes, constitute a 'feminine' language that works in opposition to Gilead's polluted technological nightmare and its accompanying rhetoric.

Gilead's official language with its texture of biblical allusions and deceit is likely to cause most problems for contemporary readers. Many of these allusions are annotated in the glossaries found in the Summaries, so here attention will be concentrated on the biblical references and their significance. Gilead's social principles are based on the Old Testament, where patriarchal authority is justified as the law of God. There are far more references to the Old than to the New Testament, a common feature of more extreme sects where the archaic language of patriarchy is used as a mechanism for social control. The patriarch Jacob is the state hero, and the name Gilead is closely associated with Jacob, for that was the place where he set up his heap of stones as witness to God and where he established his household, his lineage and his flocks and herds (see the note on Gilead on p. 11).

The first quotation in the **epigraph** directs our attention to Genesis 30:1–3, which is the beginning of the story about Jacob and his two wives Rachel and Leah and their two handmaids who are required to produce children for them. As the basis of the novel it is reiterated many times in the text, most notably in the family Bible reading before the monthly Ceremony, and there are echoes of it in the name of the Rachel and Leah Centre and in Offred's remark that *'Give me children, or else I die'* can have more than one meaning for her as a Handmaid (p. 71). As already mentioned, the New Testament is less in evidence, though there is one long passage quoted (1 Timothy 2:9–15) which is used at the mass marriage ceremony in Chapter 34 as part of Gilead's **propaganda** about male domination and female submission.

In such a society biblical references pervade every level of discourse. Gilead's leaders understand very well the importance of language as the main instrument of ideological control, and indeed it is just as repressive an instrument as the army and the police, and a great deal more insidious because rituals of naming determine the way we think about our lives. The law enforcers themselves are named after

CHECK THE BOOK

The Commandments of the Republic of Gilead are variants of the Ten Commandments in the Bible. Check Exodus 20:1–19 against Gilead's prohibitions to observe their manipulation of the originals.

Old Testament figures, whether they are 'Guardian Angels' or the 'Eyes of the Lord'. One of the most shocking features of Gilead is its abuse of language and its misappropriation of the language of the Bible, which contributes to the oppressive tone of the novel. (It reminds us of Orwell's Newspeak, where the Ministry of Truth is really the Ministry of Lies). With its **euphemisms**, neologisms, and biblical misquotations, language is destabilised, and this in turn promotes the anxieties and uncertainties which are part of daily life. It is through words that Gilead seeks to control people's minds: Aunt Lydia's slogan 'Gilead is within you' (p. 33) is blasphemy, being a parody of Christ's words 'The Kingdom of God is within you'. It shows the ways Gilead works to internalise its principles in everybody's lives.

On the domestic level, women's roles are given biblical significance, as in the case of the Handmaids, of course, but also in that of the female servants who become 'Marthas' after the woman who served Christ. (There is an amusing break in the rhetoric with the references to the 'Econowives', whose naming seems more influenced by late twentieth-century advertising than by Scripture.) With 'Jezebel's' as the name of the state-run brothel, however, Gilead's misogyny is made plain, for Jezebel's name suggests the scandal of female sexuality which Gilead can neither condone nor ignore. In a country where God is treated as a 'national resource', biblical names filter into the commercial world. The car brand names available are 'Behemoth', 'Whirlwind' or 'Chariot' (instead of 'Tigra' or 'Cobra', for example?) and shops have been renamed with pictorial signs which pick up biblical texts like 'Lilies of the Field' and 'All Flesh'. It is an **ironic** comment on the fact that such naming is only the most superficial sanctification of shopping by coupons, for everything is rationed in Gilead.

Perhaps the funniest misappropriation is Aunt Lydia's exhortation to the Handmaids, which she claims is from St Paul: 'From each according to her ability, to each according to his needs' (p. 127). These words are not in the Bible at all; they are a garbled version of Karl Marx's description of systems of production, though they do make the point that Aunt Lydia wished to stress about service roles. In a similar way the Freudian reference to 'Pen Is Envy' (p. 196) and the Miltonic reference 'They also serve …' (p. 28) also emphasise

? QUESTION
'Love is not the point'. How does Offred's narrative contradict Aunt Lydia's statement (Chapter 41)?

women's subservience to men. We may conclude that Gilead uses biblical references to underwrite patriarchal interests, but it uses them very selectively and sometimes inaccurately. The Word is in the mouths of men only, just as the Bible is kept locked up and only Commanders are allowed to read it. Even the hymns are edited, and Moira's dissenting version of 'There is a Balm in Gilead' (p. 230) is muffled in the massed choir of the Handmaids. Offred prays quite often in her own private way, saying her version of the Lord's Prayer (Chapter 30) or crying out to God in despair (Chapter 45), but again her voice is muted. Gilead's official discourse is a hybridised rhetoric which combines biblical language with traces of American capitalist phrases ('In God We Trust' is the motto on the dollar bill), Marxism and feminism. It uses and abuses the Bible in the same way as it uses the slogans of the liberal ideology it has overthrown. One hostile Old Testament reference which Gilead chooses not to use occurs in Hosea 6:8: 'Gilead is a city of wicked men, stained with footprints of blood.'

> **CONTEXT**
>
> The Eye from the American dollar bill is also used as the logo by the secret police. As Atwood noted in a 2003 interview, the Eye has just been adopted by the American right wing Homeland Security Organisation who can control people through credit card information.

CHARACTERISATION

In many ways the ideas in this **dystopian** novel are more important than the characters – and even the most psychologically complex characters like Offred and Moira are constructed in ways that emphasise their thematic significance in the novel. The other characters tend to function as members of groups or as representatives of certain ideological positions. However, as Offred insists, every individual is significant, whatever Gilead decrees, and her narrative weaves in particularities: she continually writes in other voices in sections of dialogue, in embedded stories and in remembered episodes. It is a feature of Atwood's realism, even within a fabricated futuristic world, that she pays close attention not only to location but to people and relationships.

OFFRED

Offred, the main protagonist and narrator, is trapped in Gilead as a Handmaid, one of the 'two-legged wombs' (p. 146), valued only for her potential as a surrogate mother. Denied all her individual rights, she is known only by the patronymic Of-Fred, derived from the name of her current Commander. Most of the time she is isolated and afraid. Virtually imprisoned in the domestic spaces of the home, she is allowed out only with a shopping partner and for Handmaids' official excursions like Prayvaganzas and Salvagings. At the age of thirty-three and potentially still fertile, she is a victim of Gileadean sexist ideology which equates 'male' with power and sexual potency, and 'female' with reproduction and submission to the point where individuality is effaced. Offred's narrative, however, does not possess such diagrammatic simplicity, for she resists such reductiveness by a variety of stratagems that allow her to retain a sense of her own individuality and psychological freedom. She refuses to forget her past or her own name when she was a daughter, lover, wife and working mother; she refuses to believe in biological reductionism; and she refuses to give up hope of getting out of her present situation. She knows what she needs to pay attention to: 'What I need is perspective. The illusion of depth ... Otherwise you live in the moment. Which is not where I want to be' (p. 153).

? QUESTION
In what ways can Offred's tale be described as a resistance narrative, when she herself is neither a member of Mayday nor an obvious social dissident?

Offred's greatest psychological resource is her faculty of double vision, for she is a survivor from the past, and it is her power to remember which enables her to survive in the present. It is not only through **flashbacks** that she reconstructs the past (though these are her most effective escape routes from isolation, loneliness and boredom), but even when she walks down the road she sees everything through a double exposure, with the past superimposed upon the present, or to use her own layered image from Chapter 1, as a **palimpsest** where the past gives depth to the present. She has perfected the technique of simultaneously inhabiting two spaces: her Handmaid's space (or lack of it) and the freer, happier spaces of memory. Though she is forbidden to use her own name, she keeps it like a buried treasure, as guarantee of her other identity: 'I keep the knowledge of this name like something hidden, some treasure I'll come back to dig up, one day' (p. 94). She gives her real name as a love token to Nick, and he in turn uses it as an exchange of faith when he comes for her with the black truck: 'He calls me by my real name. Why should this mean anything?' (p. 305). Offred does not trust the reader with her real name, however, which is a sign of her wariness in a precarious situation, though it has been suggested by several critics that her real name, as coded into the text, is June. Atwood deliberately leaves it unspecific, like the date of Offred's birth or the exact dates of narrative events.

What is most attractive about Offred is her lively responsiveness to the world around her. She is sharply observant of physical details in her surroundings, she is curious and likes to explore, and she has a very lyrical response to the Commander's Wife's beautiful garden. She observes its seasonal changes closely, for that garden represents for her all the natural fecundity and beauty that are denied by the regime but which flourish unchecked outside the window. It is also a silent testimonial to her own resistance: 'There is something subversive about this garden of Serena's, a sense of buried things bursting upwards, wordlessly, into the light' (p. 161). Her response to the moonlight is equally imaginative, though noticeably tinged with **irony**, which is one of her most distinctive characteristics: 'a wishing moon, a sliver of ancient rock, a goddess, a wink. The moon is a stone and the sky is full of deadly hardware, but oh God, how beautiful anyway' (p. 108).

Offred consistently refuses to be bamboozled by the **rhetoric** of Gilead, for she believes in the principle of making distinctions between things and in the precise use of words, just as she continues to believe in the value of every individual. Of the men in her life she says: 'Each one remains unique, there is no way of joining them together. They cannot be exchanged, one for the other. They cannot replace each other' (p. 202).

It is this sharpness of mind which informs her wittily critical view of her present situation, as in the satisfaction she gets out of teasing the young guard at the gate. 'I enjoy the power; power of a dog bone, passive but there' (p. 32). Her attitude is discreetly subversive but never openly rebellious. She watches for those moments of instability which she calls 'tiny peepholes' (p. 31) when human responses break through official surfaces. Offred is mischievous, but, more seriously, she yearns for communication and trust between people instead of mutual suspicion and isolation. **Ironically** enough, her fullest human relationship in Gilead is her 'arrangement' with the Commander. 'The fact is that I'm his mistress' (p. 172). This is where 'taboo dissolved' (p. 165), for it is in their Scrabble games that Offred is at her liveliest and her most conventionally feminine. In his study, Offred and the Commander relate to each other by old familiar social and sexual codes, which alleviates the loneliness both feel. It is after her first evening that

CHECK THE BOOK

Commenting on Offred's narrative, Atwood said: 'You're dealing with a character whose ability to move in the society was limited. She was boxed in... the more limited and boxed in you are, the more important details become. If you are in jail in solitary, the advent of a rat can be pretty important to you.' See *Margaret Atwood, Conversations*, p. 216.

Offred does something she has never done before in the novel: she laughs out loud, partly at the absurdity of it all, but partly out of a reawakening of her own high spirits. Yet she is too intelligent ever to forget that it is only a game or a replay of the past in **parodic** form, and her outing to Jezebel's confirms this. For all its glitter, her purple sequined costume, like the evening, is a shabby masquerade, and in the clear light of day she is left sitting with 'a handful of crumpled stars' in her lap (p. 303).

> **QUESTION**
> 'I've tried to put some of the good things in as well. Flowers, for instance.' Discuss Offred's vocabulary of images in the light of her statement.

Living in a terrorist state, Offred is always alert to the glint of danger, as in her first unexpected encounter with Nick in the dark where fear and sexual risk exert a powerful charge which runs through the novel to its end. Their love represents the forbidden combination of desire and rebellion, and it is through that relationship that Offred manages to find new hope for the future and even to accommodate herself to reduced circumstances in the present, like a pioneer who has given up the Old World and come to the wilderness of a new one: 'I said, I have made a life for myself, here, of a sort. That must have been what the settlers' wives thought' (p. 283). Offred shows through her detailed psychological narrative how she can survive traumas of loss and bereavement and how she manages to elude the constraints of absolute authority. We know little about her physical appearance because the only time she ever mentions it is when she is at her most bizarre, in her red habit with her white winged cap or in her purple sequined costume at Jezebel's. But we know a great deal about her mind and feelings and her sense of wry humour. We also know that she is a highly **self-conscious narrator** and that she is aware of contradictions and failings within herself. She knows that she lacks Moira's flamboyant courage, and she accuses herself of cowardice and unreliability, just as at the end she feels guilty for having betrayed the household who imprisoned her. Yet, despite her own self-doubts, Offred manages to convince us of her integrity. She survives with dignity and a measure of self-respect as she embraces the possibility of her escape with hope. She is a new kind of heroine, who wins the battle against the numbing and often dangerous practicalities of everyday life, and her narrative remains a witness to the freedom and resilience of the human spirit. She lingers in the reader's memory like 'a wraith of red smoke' (p. 219).

Offred and Moira are the two main examples of feminist positions in the novel (unlike the older women Serena Joy and the Aunts). Yet they are very different from each other, for Offred's resistance always works surreptitiously and through compromise, whereas Moira is more confrontational. Offred represents Atwood's version of a moderate heterosexual feminism in contrast to Moira's separatist feminism.

MOIRA

Moira, always known by her own name because she never becomes a Handmaid, is strongly individual, although she is also a type of the female rebel. This is a position which can be viewed in two ways, and both of them are illustrated here. From Offred's point of view Moira is the embodiment of female heroism, though from the Gileadean authorities' point of view she is a 'loose woman', a criminal element, and her story follows the conventional fictional pattern of such rebellious figures: when Offred last sees her she is working as a prostitute in Jezebel's. Even here, Moira manages to express her dissidence, for she remains a declared lesbian and her costume is a deliberate travesty of feminine sexual allure, as Offred notices when she meets her again on her night out with the Commander. Moira's own wryly comic comment on it is, 'I guess they thought it was me' (p. 254).

> **CONTEXT**
>
> In Atwood's critical history of North American feminism, Moira represents the individualistic and pluralised feminisms of the late 1980s and 1990s which include the different agendas of formerly marginalised groups of women: Black women and lesbians whose interests are closer to Gay Rights than to traditionally liberal feminist agendas of an earlier generation.

Moira, too, is a survivor of the American permissive society, a trendy college student who wears purple overalls and leaves her unfinished paper on 'Date Rape' to go for a beer. Much more astute about sexual politics than Offred, she is an activist in the Gay Rights movement, working for a women's collective at the time of the Gilead coup. When she is brought into the Rachel and Leah Centre she is still wearing jeans and declares that the place is a 'loony bin' (p. 81). She cannot be terrorised into even outward conformity; instead she tries to escape and succeeds on her second attempt. She manages to escape disguised as an Aunt. Always funny and ironic, to the other women at the Centre she represents all that they would like to do but would not dare: 'Moira was our fantasy. We hugged her to us, she was with us in secret, a giggle; she was lava beneath the crust of daily life. In the light of Moira, the Aunts were less fearsome and more absurd' (p. 143).

MOIRA continued

CHECK THE BOOK

Lee Briscoe Thompson in *Scarlet Letters* describes Moira as Offred's 'rebel alter ego' (p. 39), highlighting the contrast between two types of female heroism.

Moira continues to surface in Offred's narrative, bobbing up in memory, until her devastatingly funny final appearance at Jezebel's. Behind the comedy, however, is the fact that Moira has not managed to escape after all, and as an unregenerate has been consigned to the brothel, where she tells Offred that she has 'three or four good years' (p. 261) ahead of her, drinking and smoking as a Jezebel hostess, before she is sent to the Colonies. Our last view of Moira is on that evening: 'I'd like her to end with something daring and spectacular, some outrage, something that would befit her. But as far as I know that didn't happen' (p. 262).

Moira is one of the spirited feminist heroines, like Offred's mother and Offred's predecessor in the Commander's house who left the message scrawled in the closet. The sad fact is these women do get sent off to the Colonies or commit suicide, which Offred herself refuses to do. Offred and Moira are both feminist heroines, showing women's energetic resistance to the Gilead system, but there are no winners. Neither compromise nor rebellion wins freedom, though it is likely that Offred is rescued by Nick. However, their value lies in their speaking out against the imposition of silence, challenging tyranny and oppression. Their stories highlight the actions of two individual women whose very different private assertions become exemplary or **symbolic**. Their voices survive as images of hope and defiance to be vindicated by history.

SERENA JOY

Serena Joy, the Commander's Wife, is the most powerful female presence in Offred's daily life in Gilead, and as Offred has plenty of opportunity to observe her at close quarters she appears in the narrative as more than just a member of a class in the hierarchy of Gileadean women. Significantly, unlike all the other wives, she is referred to by her own name. As an elderly childless woman she has to agree to the grotesque system of polygamy practised in Gilead and to shelter a Handmaid in her home, but it is plain that she resents this arrangement keenly as a violation of her marriage, and a continual reminder of her own crippled condition and fading feminine charms. The irony of the situation is made clear when Offred remembers Serena Joy's past history, first as a child singing star on a gospel television show, and later as a media personality speaking up for ultra-conservative domestic policies and the sanctity

QUESTION In what ways is Serena Joy a significant presence in the novel?

of the home. Now, as Offred maliciously remarks, Serena is trapped in the very ideology on which she had based her popularity: 'She stays in her home, but it doesn't seem to agree with her' (p. 56).

Serena's present life is a parody of the Virtuous Woman: her only place of power is her own living room, she is estranged from her husband, jealous of her Handmaid, and has nothing to do except knit scarves for soldiers and gossip with her cronies or listen to her young voice on the gramophone. The only space for Serena's self-expression is her garden, and even that she cannot tend without the help of her husband's chauffeur. If flowers are important to Offred, so are they too to Serena, and she often sits alone in her 'subversive garden', knitting or smoking or viciously cutting off the heads of flowers.

To see the world from Serena's perspective is to shift the emphasis of Offred's narrative, for these two women might be seen not as opposites but as **doubles**. They both want a child, and the attention of them both focuses on the Commander of whom Serena is very possessive: 'As for my husband, she said, he's just that. My husband. I want that to be perfectly clear. Till death do us part. It's final' (p. 26).

Offred seldom knows what Serena is thinking, though there are indications of her attitudes and tastes in the jewels and the perfume she wears and in the furnishings of her house: 'hard lust for quality, soft sentimental cravings' as Offred uncharitably puts it (p. 90). There is also evidence of a certain toughness in Serena's cigarette-smoking and her use of slang, not to mention her suggestion that Offred, unknown to the Commander, should sleep with Nick in order to conceive the child she is supposed to produce: 'She's actually smiling, coquettishly even; there's a hint of her former small-screen mannequin's allure, flickering over her face like momentary static' (p. 216). But Serena has her revenges too: she has deliberately withheld from Offred the news of her lost daughter and her photograph which Offred has been longing for.

By a curious twist, Serena occupies the role of the wife in a very conventional plot about marital infidelity, as well as in the privileged Gileadean sense. She is one of the points in the triangular relationship which develops between Offred and the Commander:

> **CONTEXT**
>
> Serena Joy is a satirical portrait, a composite of several Christian Right wives who were media personalities in the early 1980s: Tammy Faye Bakker, who with her husband ran a gospel television show; Phyllis Schlafly, a lawyer who campaigned for women's return to the home; Beverley LaHaye, who organised demonstrations against abortions and the ERA.

'The fact is that I'm his mistress ... Sometimes I think she knows' (p. 172). Actually, she does not know until she finds the purple costume and the lipstick on her cloak. It is a cliché-like situation, but Serena's own pain of loss goes beyond this conventional pattern: '"Behind my back," she says. "You could have left me something."' Offred wonders, 'Does she love him, after all?' (p. 299).

Serena is still there in her house, standing anxiously beside the Commander at the end as Offred is led out through the door. Her farewell to Offred is wifely in an old-fashioned sense which has none of the pieties of Gilead: '"Bitch," she says. "After all he did for you"' (p. 307).

THE OTHER COMMANDERS' WIVES

These merely exist as a gaggle of gossips in blue, for Offred knows nothing of their lives apart from overhearing snatches of their conversation at Birth Days, Prayvaganzas or social visits, when they make scandalous comments about their Handmaids. Only the Wife of Warren achieves a moment of grotesque individuality when she is seen sitting on the Birth Stool behind Janine, 'wearing white cotton socks, and bedroom slippers, blue ones made of fuzzy material, like toilet-seat covers' (p. 135). There is also one other unfortunate Wife who is hanged at the Salvaging, but Offred does not know what her crime was. Was it murder? Was it adultery? 'It could always be that. Or attempted escape' (p. 287).

THE AUNTS

Like the Wives, the Marthas, the Econowives and most of the Handmaids, these are presented as members of a class or group, every group representing a different female role within Gilead. With their names derived from pre-Gileadean women's products, the Aunts are the older women who act as female collaborators on the orders of the patriarchy to train and police Handmaids. Their names suggest cakes and cosmetics, for example, Aunt Elizabeth (Elizabeth Arden cosmetics). Aunt Sara (Sara Lee cakes), Aunt Helena (Helena Rubenstein cosmetics). An alternative explanation is that many of the Aunts' names are biblical: Lydia was a rich woman converted to Christianity by St Paul (Acts 16:14); Elizabeth was the mother of John the Baptist (Luke 1:23-25); Sara was the wife of Abraham who

CONTEXT

The practice of depriving people of their names and so robbing them of individual identities to emphasise their interchangeability has a long history – in slavery, colonial practices, and more recently in Nazi concentration camps.

conceived a son in her old age (Genesis 21:1-5). They are a
paramilitary organisation, as is signified by their khaki uniforms and
their cattle prods, and, as propagandists of the regime, they tell
distorted tales of women's lives in the pre-Gileadean past. The
villainesses of the novel, they are responsible for the most gruesome
cruelties, like the female Salvagings and the Particicutions, as well as
for individual punishments at the Rachel and Leah Centre.

Only Aunt Lydia is individuated, and that is by her peculiar
viciousness masquerading under a genteel feminine exterior: 'Aunt
Lydia thought she was very good at feeling for other people' (p. 56).
A particularly sadistic tormentor, Aunt Lydia is an awful warning
that a women's culture is no guarantee of sisterhood as Offred's
mother's generation of feminists had optimistically assumed, but
that it is also necessary to take account of some women's
pathological inclinations towards violence and vindictiveness.

OFGLEN AND OFWARREN

Only two of the Handmaids, Ofglen and Ofwarren (Janine), emerge
as individuals, one because of her courage and rebelliousness and
the other because she is the conventional female victim figure. Both
are casualties of the Gileadean system.

Ofglen has no past life that Offred knows about, but she does have a
secret life as a member of the Mayday resistance movement which
she confides to Offred after weeks as her shopping partner. There is
nothing exceptional about her appearance except her mechanical
quality which Offred notices, 'as if she's voice-activated, as if she's
on little oiled wheels' (p. 53). Offred is proved right in her
suspicions, for under the disguise of Handmaid, Ofglen is a sturdy
resistance fighter. She identifies the alleged rapist as 'one of ours' and
knocks him out before the horrible Particicution begins. She also
dies as a fighter, preferring to commit suicide when she sees the black
truck coming rather than betray her friends under torture. Offred
learns this from her replacement, the 'new, treacherous Ofglen', who
whispers the news to her on their shopping expedition.

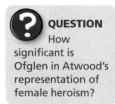

Janine is a female victim in both her lives: before Gilead when she
worked as a waitress and was raped by a gang of thugs, then as a
Handmaid. At the Rachel and Leah Centre she is a craven figure on

the edge of nervous collapse, and consequently one of Aunt Lydia's pets. Though she has her moment of triumph as the 'vastly pregnant' (p. 36) Handmaid Ofwarren in Chapter 5, she is also a victim of the system with which she has tried so hard to curry favour. Even at the Birth Day she is neglected as soon as the baby is born and left 'crying helplessly, burnt-out miserable tears' when her baby is taken away and given to the Wife (p. 137). There is no reward for Janine. Her baby is declared an Unbaby and destroyed because it is deformed; Janine becomes a pale shadow overwhelmed with guilt; finally, after the Particicution, when Offred sees her again, she has slipped over into madness.

OFFRED'S MOTHER

Offred's mother and her life belong to the history of feminism which is being recorded in this novel, for she joined the Women's Liberation Movement of the 1960s and 1970s, campaigning for women's sexual and social freedom. As an older woman she continued to be a political activist, and at the time of the Gileadean takeover she disappeared. Only much later does Offred learn that she has been condemned as an Unwoman and sent to the Colonies.

CONTEXT

Second wave feminism takes as its starting point the politics of reproduction, while sharing first wave feminism's politics of legal, educational and economic equal rights for women,' see Maggie Humm, *Feminisms*, p. 53.

Like Moira, and possessing the same kind of energy, Offred's mother resists classification. In an odd way she even resists being dead, for she makes two startling appearances in the present, both times on film at the Rachel and Leah Centre. On one occasion Offred is shocked to see her as a young woman marching toward her in a pro-abortion march, and later Moira reports seeing her as an old woman working as slave labour in the Colonies.

Offred's mother is, however, more than a feminist icon. She haunts her daughter's memory, and gradually Offred comes to understand her mother's independence of mind and to admire her courage. Her mother is evoked in a series of kaleidoscopic images: at a feminist pornographic book burning (Chapter 7), with a bruised face after an abortion riot (Chapter 28), and as an elderly woman proudly defending her position as a single parent to Offred's husband, while accusing her daughter of naïveté and political irresponsibility. It is her jaunty language which Offred remembers as distinguishing her mother:

A man is just a woman's strategy for making other women. Not that your father wasn't a nice guy and all, but he wasn't up to fatherhood. Not that I expected it of him. Just do the job, then you can bugger off, I said, I make a decent salary, I can afford daycare. So he went to the coast and sent Christmas cards. He had beautiful blue eyes though.   (p. 131)

An embarrassing but heroic figure, this is the woman whom her daughter misses when it is all too late, though Offred continues her dialogue with her mother in her own mind as a way of keeping her alive: 'Mother, I think. Wherever you may be. Can you hear me? You wanted a women's culture. Well, now there is one. It isn't what you meant, but it exists. Be thankful for small mercies' (p. 137).

Finally Offred tries to lay her mother to rest, but without success: 'I've mourned for her already. But I will do it again, and again' (p. 265).

Deprived of the freedoms which her mother fought for, Offred learns to admire her mother's courage and to value her memory as a vital link with her own lost identity. Her elegy to her mother underlines the thematic motif of Missing Persons, and particularly lost mothers and daughters, which runs through the novel.

MALE CHARACTERS

The few male characters in this novel seem little more than functionaries of the patriarchal state or functional to the workings of the plot. Most of them have no names but only group identities like 'Angels' or 'Eyes' or 'the doctor', while Professor Pieixoto is a **satirical** sketch of a male academic. Only three male characters are given any individuating characteristics. They are Offred's Commander, her lover Nick, and her absent, vanished husband Luke.

THE COMMANDER

The Commander is the most powerful authority figure in Offred's world. He is a high-ranking government official, and he is head of the household to which Offred is assigned. It is his first name which she takes, though whether as a slave or as a **parody** of the marriage service is never made clear. Yet he is an ambiguous figure, substantial but shadowy, whose motivations, like his career in Gilead, remain

> **? QUESTION**
> To what extent does the portrayal of Offred's mother draw a dangerous parallel between her militant feminism and the absolutism of the fundamentalist Christian Right?

unclear to Offred; even in the 'Historical Notes' his identity remains uncertain. As a Commander he wears a black uniform and is driven in a prestige car, a Whirlwind. He is an elderly man with 'straight neatly brushed silver hair' and a moustache and blue eyes. He is slightly stooped and his manner is mild (p. 97). As Offred observes him with his gold-rimmed glasses on his nose reading from the Bible before the monthly Ceremony, she thinks he looks 'like a midwestern bank president' (p. 97) an astute judgment, as he tells her much later that before Gilead he was in market research (p. 195). The image he presents is that of male power, isolated and benignly indifferent to domestic matters, which include his Wife and his Handmaid. This is, however, not entirely true, for Offred has seen him earlier on the day of the Ceremony, a figure lurking in the shadows outside her room, who tried to peer at her as she passed: 'Something has been shown to me, but what is it?' (p. 59).

CONTEXT

Bluebeard was a murderous tyrant in Charles Perrault's *Contes du Temps* (1697). In Perrault's tale, Bluebeard entrusts the key to his castle to his new wife, forbidding her to enter one of the rooms. But left on her own, she unlocks the door to find it full of the dead bodies of his former wives.

It is only after the official Ceremony, performed by the Commander in full dress uniform and with his eyes shut, that Offred has the chance to get to know him a little and his stereotypical male power image begins to break down. It is he who asks her to visit him 'after hours' in his study, for he is a lonely man who desires friendship and intimacy with his Handmaid and not the serviceable monthly sex for which she has been allocated to him. In his Bluebeard's chamber, what he has to offer is not 'kinky sex' but Scrabble games and an appearance of 'normal life', with conversation and books and magazines, all of which he knows are forbidden to Handmaids. On his own private territory the Commander is an old-fashioned gentleman with an attractive sheepish smile, who treats Offred in a genially patronising way and gradually becomes quite fond of her. 'In fact he is positively daddyish' (p. 193). He seems to have the ability to compartmentalise his life (in a way that Offred cannot manage) so that he can separate her official role as sexual slave from her unofficial role as his companion. In many ways the Commander's motives and needs remain obscure to Offred, though they do manage to develop an amiable relationship, which from one point of view is bizarre and from another is entirely banal: 'The fact is that I'm his mistress' (p. 172).

Yet their relationship is still a game of sexual power politics in which the Commander holds most of the cards, as Offred never allows herself to forget. For all his gallantry, he remains totally trapped in traditional patriarchal assumptions, believing that these are 'Nature's norm' (p. 232) and allow exploitation of women, as his comments and conduct at Jezebel's suggest. Their private sexual encounter there ends in 'futility and bathos' (p. 267) and is strongly contrasted with Offred's meeting with Nick later that same evening. As she leaves his house for the last time, Offred sees the Commander standing at the living-room door, looking old, worried and helpless. Possibly he is expecting his own downfall, for nobody is invulnerable in Gilead. Offred has her revenge, for the balance of power between them has shifted: 'Possibly he will be a security risk, now. I am above him, looking down; he is shrinking' (p. 306).

The academics go to some trouble later to establish the Commander's identity: he may have been 'Frederick R. Waterford' or 'B. Frederick Judd'. Waterford, it is revealed, had a background in market research (which seems most likely), while the more sinister Judd was a military strategist who worked for the CIA. Both of them 'met their ends, probably soon after the events our author describes'(pp. 321–2). Gilead, like Orwell's Oceania, was in the habit of shredding documents in order to revise the official version of state history.

? **QUESTION**
How does Atwood define the word 'political' in this novel? Consider how its meanings are worked out through her exploration of power and resistance in private and public relations.

NICK

Nick is presented as the central figure of Offred's romantic fantasy, for he is the mysterious dark stranger who is her rescuer through love. He also has a place in her real world, of course, as the Commander's chauffeur and the Commander's Wife's gardener. He 'has a French face, lean, whimsical, all planes and angles, with creases around the mouth where he smiles' (p. 28) and a general air of irreverence, wearing his cap at a jaunty angle, whistling while he polishes the car, and winking at Offred the first day he sees her. At the household prayers he presses his foot against hers, and she feels a surge of sensual warmth which she dare not acknowledge. In the daytime he is rather a comic figure but at night he is transformed into Offred's romantic lover, the embodiment of sexual desire. This transformation is made all the more piquant because he is always acting under orders, either as the Commander's messenger or as the lover chosen for Offred by the Commander's Wife.

**CHECK
THE BOOK**

For a short lyric account of what falling in love feels like, read Atwood's poem which begins: 'Nothing like love to put blood in the language,' in *Eating Fire*, p. 249.

From their first unexpected encounter in the dark living room (Chapter 17) theirs is a silent exchange which carries an unmistakable erotic charge. It is Nick's hands which make his declaration: 'His fingers move, feeling my arm under the night-gown sleeve, as if his hand won't listen to reason. It's so good, to be touched by someone, to be felt so greedily, to feel so greedy' (p. 110).

As a subordinate, Nick, like Offred, has to remain passive until ordered by the Commander's Wife to go to bed with Offred. On that occasion his attitude is not directly described but veiled by Offred's three different versions of that meeting. Certainly she falls in love with him, and in defiance of danger she returns many times to his room across the dark lawn on her own. Towards the end, she tells him that she is pregnant. Nevertheless, her description of their lovemaking is suggestive rather than explicitly erotic, and Nick tends to remain a mysterious figure.

Even at the end when he appears with the Eyes to take her away, Offred really knows so little about him that she almost accuses him of having betrayed her, until he calls her by her real name and begs her to trust him. Ever elusive, he is the only member of the household not there to see her depart. We want to believe that Nick was in love with Offred, and we must assume from the 'Historical Notes' that he did rescue her and that he was a member of Mayday resistance. However, as a character he is very lightly sketched and it is his function as romantic lover which is most significant. Nick is more important for his role than as a realistic character, for he belongs to romance rather than to realism. Their relationship is significant for underlining Offred's powerful conflict of loyalties and the strength of her sexual desire which comes to outweigh her loyalty to Luke and even her desire to escape.

LUKE

Luke, Offred's husband, is one of the Missing Persons in this novel. Probably dead before the narrative begins, he haunts Offred's memory until he fades like a ghost as her love affair with Nick develops. He is the one person Offred leaves out when she tells the story of her past life to Nick (Chapter 41), though she is still worrying about him at the end (Chapter 44).

He is also the most fragmented character in the text, appearing briefly as a name in Chapter 2, and then gradually taking on an identity as Offred's lover, husband and the father of her child. He is a figure whose life story stopped for Offred at a traumatic point in the past: 'Stopped dead in time, in mid-air, among the trees back there, in the act of falling' (p. 239). Through her reconstruction Luke appears as a late twentieth-century 'liberated man', full of courage and humour and remembered by Offred entirely in his domestic relations with her. He is an older man who has been married before, so that there is an **ironic** parallel drawn between him and the Commander. Offred remembers their affair when she goes with the Commander to Jezebel's, for it is the hotel where she and Luke used to go (Chapter 37). She retains the memory of a strong loving partner, and her detailed recollections are of Luke cooking and joking with her mother, of lying in bed with her before their daughter was born, of collecting their daughter from school. We never know what Luke's job was, but Offred recalls his supportive behaviour when she lost her job at the time of the Gileadean takeover and her resentment against him for being a man (Chapter 28).

Luke figures insistently in Offred's recurring nightmare of their failed escape attempt, not only in that final image of him lying shot face down in the snow, but also in her recollections of his careful preparations and his coolly courageous attempt to take his family to freedom over the Canadian border. His afterlife in the novel is very much the result of Offred's anxieties about what might have happened to him. Is he dead, or in prison? Did he escape? Will he send her a message and help her to escape back into their old family life? 'It's this message, which may never arrive, that keeps me alive. I believe in the message' (p. 116). It is also her hope of this message which keeps the image of Luke alive. The anxieties we may feel for his fate are projections of Offred's own.

? QUESTION
'Some people think that the society in The Handmaid's Tale is one in which all men have power, and all women don't. That is not true.' M. Atwood, 2001. Investigate the key features of gender politics in this novel.

? QUESTION
'The Handmaid's Tale' brings out the very best in Atwood – moral vision, biting humour, and a poet's imagination.' Do you agree or disagree with this statement?

PART FOUR

CRITICAL HISTORY

A great deal of attention has been paid to *The Handmaid's Tale* as **dystopian** science fiction (or speculative fiction as Atwood prefers to call it) and as a novel of feminist protest. It has won many prizes, notably the Arthur C. Clarke Science Fiction Prize, and has been made into a film directed by Volker Schlondorff and starring Natasha Richardson, Faye Dunaway, and Robert Duvall. Most recently it has been made into an opera by the Danish composer Poul Ruders in 2000, which had its English language premiere in London in 2003. Yet the novel has provoked criticism in America from the religious right and aroused some debate over Atwood's exposure of the flaws and failures of 'second wave' feminism, especially in her representation of the Aunts and the character of Offred. Indeed, Atwood is not exclusively concerned with feminist politics but rather with gender politics and with basic human rights. *The Handmaid's Tale* has become a cultural reference point as it brings into focus many of the anxieties and fears of contemporary Western society as well as assuming an almost prophetic quality as events in the real world rush in to confirm its predictions: 'The book seems ever more relevant in a world of jostling theocracies and diminished civil liberties in both east and west' (*Guardian Review*, 26 April, 2003, p. 23). As one interviewer phrased it in 2001: 'It's almost impossible now to imagine a time when *The Handmaid's Tale* didn't exist.'

Looking back to its first publication in 1985, the reviews voiced a conflicting range of responses (which may be related to the different nationalities of the reviewers). As Atwood commented:

> In my native Canada, response from media people was a nervous, 'could it happen here?' In England, the book was treated more as a good yarn than as social realism ... But in the United States, where these motifs were close to home, they didn't even use the word 'could'. Instead, it was, 'How long have we got, and how can we prevent it?' ('The Handmaid's Tale – Before and After')

 CHECK THE NET

For a listing of manuscript materials relating to this novel, see website of Thomas Fisher Rare Book Library, University of Toronto **http://www.library. utoronto.ca/fisher/ atwood The Handmaid's Tale** materials are in Box 96.

These disparities are reflected in the reviews, as my selection suggests. The first one is Canadian, the second is British, and the last three are American:

(1) In *The Handmaid's Tale*, Atwood's pessimism comes to the fore as she attempts to frighten us into an awareness of our destiny before it's too late (*Globe and Mail*, 1985).

(2) Atwood's triumph is to capture the eerily static, minute-by-minute quality of Offred's sensations, in a life reduced to a meagre sequence of small incidents and stifled and impoverished human contacts, and seen through a consciousness heightened by waiting and fear (*London Review of Books*, 1986).

(3) She gives us far too little action and far too much of the longueurs long suffered by the interned Offred (*USA Today*, 1986).

(4) The novel achieves what it is meant to do, shatters complacency and pulls us up short (*Detroit Free Press*, 1986).

(5) *The Handmaid's Tale* provides a compelling lesson in power politics and in reasonable intentions gone hysteric (*Philadelphia Inquirer*, 1986).

These reviews map out the initial critical approaches to the novel, with their emphases on genre and gender – *The Handmaid's Tale* as dystopia and the fact that it is a feminist dystopia, where as the Commander explains to Offred: 'Better never means better for everyone … It always means worse, for some' (p. 222). In Gilead, 'some' principally means 'women'. Offred's first-person narrative was not universally read as feminist protest but rather as a female victim's cry of desperation, though two male reviewers (one English and one American) did tune in appreciatively to Offred's humorously **ironic** voice:

CHECK THE BOOK

See Lee Briscoe Thompson's *Scarlet Letters* for a comprehensive list of quotations from contemporary reviews (pp. 78–82), from which I have made a small selection.

> Gripping like an intelligent thriller, compelling like all believable dystopias, it's also a reply to puritans of left and right, showing how, even in conditions of dire psychic deprivation, people still want and get sex. It's a sign of life, indestructible (*New Statesman*, 1987).

And

> Atwood's book is suffused by life – the heroine's irrepressible vitality and the author's lovely subversive hymn to our ordinary life, as lived, amid perils and pollution, now. (*New Yorker*, 1986)

Of course, the dystopian theme has remained high on the agenda of critical approaches. Atwood's 1998 lectures in France on 'The Genesis of *The Handmaid's Tale* and the Role of the Historical Notes' (*The Handmaid's Tale, roman protéen*, ed. J-M. Lacroix, J. Leclaire and J. Warwick) and on '*The Handmaid's Tale*: A Feminist Dystopia?' (*Lire Margaret Atwood: The Handmaid's Tale*, ed. M. Dvorak) describes in detail the origins of her book, while her important website discussion of the novel (referred to on p. 12 and p. 38) highlights the contemporary and historical contexts out of which she constructed her disaster scenario of the near future. Of the many critical essays discussing her dystopia in the feminine, two might be mentioned for the different emphases. Lynette Hunter's essay in M.Dvorak's collection highlights the differences between Orwells' *Nineteen Eighty-Four* and *The Handmaid's Tale*: 'If Orwell's focus is on the strategies of state control and their effect on individuals still struggling to remain separate from that control, Atwood's focus is on the extent to which the individual can push at the limits of social determinism. The difference underlines the different perspective offered by each text, the former with a focus on the construction of state control, and the latter with a focus on the activity of the individual within that control' (Dvorak, pp. 23-25). C.A. Howells's essay on 'Transgressing Genre: A Generic Approach to Atwood's Novels' (*Margaret Atwood: Works and Impact*, ed. R.Nischik) focuses on the difference the narrator's gender makes to the telling of history: 'Offred is marginalised and disempowered because of her sex, so that her story shifts the structural relations between the private and public worlds of the dystopia, where the officially silenced Other becomes the central narrative voice' (Nischik, p. 142).

This second essay is indicative of the changes in critical approaches to the novel since the mid 1990s, where the major focus has shifted to Offred as narrator and her powers of resistance to patriarchal tyranny through storytelling. The emphasis is on questions of narrative technique, focusing on **postmodern** elements in the text.

 CHECK THE NET

Asked about her research for *The Handmaid's Tale*, Atwood says 'there isn't anything in the book not based on something that has already happened in history . . .'. See **www.randomhouse. com** for a full explanation.

What kind of story does she tell and what kind of language does she use? She has been seen as a Scheherazade figure, reconstructing her life as a feminine subject who eludes her victim status, just as she reconstructs her 'little' life narrative in opposition to the 'grand' narrative of Gileadean imperialism. Critics are paying increasing attention to the gendered signs within this woman's life writing, such as her language of the body and of female desire.

Atwood has always insisted on the importance of Offred as narrator and on storytelling as her means of resistance to the oppressions of her Handmaid's role: 'It's the story of one woman under this regime, told in a very personal way, and part of the challenge for me was the creation of her voice and viewpoint'('The Handmaid's Tale – Before and After'). This is after all a woman's survival narrative, where Offred lays claim to many things forbidden by Gilead – to her own name, her room, her memories of the past. She tells her story in a confessional mode, as Sherrill Grace's essay on 'Gender as Genre' (*Margaret Atwood: Writing and Subjectivity*, ed. C. Nicholson) explores in detail: 'What Offred sets before us in this autobiography is her desperate struggle to reconstruct her being across an all but unbridgeable, violent severing of time before and after the imposition of Gilead. To do this she must insist upon her own script in a world where her voice has been erased' (p. 196). Grace discusses the significance of the Scrabble game as a play with words and she also pays attention to the narrative pattern where accumulated details of daily life are regularly interspersed with the meditative 'Night' sections. Finally she analyses the 'Historical Notes', in the Professor's attempt to erase Offred's voice again in the future.

CONTEXT

Conflicting interpretations and revisionary readings of this novel testify to its relevance in changing contemporary contexts. As Atwood explained: 'You cannot determine people's reactions to your book. If it's a book with any power, there's always going to be some form of uproar.'

Grace's analysis is supplemented by Lee Thompson's discussion in *Scarlet Letters* of some of the postmodern elements of Offred's storytelling: 'Early on Offred realises the complexities of the relationship among story, teller, and listener, as well as the ambiguities of the boundaries between story and truth' (p. 60). It was Linda Hutcheon in *The Canadian Postmodern* who first highlighted Offred's narrative self consciousness with her close scrutiny of her own motives for storytelling as she attempts to stay sane in what Moira describes as a 'loony bin' (p. 81): 'The narrator self-consciously tries to tell her story (a true one, but also, she

CRITICAL HISTORY

 CHECK THE BOOK

Dvorak uses Offred's own words when describing the novel: 'This is a reconstruction ... It's a reconstruction now, in my head, as I lie flat in my single bed' (p. 144).

realises, inevitably ordered, constructed, fictionalised' (p. 156). This is a world where 'men still rule; women still collude.' (Is Hutcheon describing Gilead, or is she referring to our own world - or to both fiction and real life?) Marta Dvorak's essay 'What's in a Name' *Lire (Margaret Atwood: The Handmaid's Tale/Le Conte de la servante: the Power Game*, eds. J-M. Lacroix and J. Leclaire) adopts a postmodern approach when she argues that Offred's story shows how 'our ideology or visions of the world are socially constructed, and as such, may be transformed or reconstructed' (p. 81). She also analyses some of the 'booby traps' in the novel which break the realistic illusion.

This critical concern with postmodern narrative techniques is complemented by recent feminist approaches. Here topics focus on issues like female sexuality, mothers and daughters, sisterhood and the Aunts' role. However, the main emphasis is on Offred's writing about her female body, her sensations and her desires. All these critics allude to Hélène Cixous' pioneering essay 'The Laugh of the Medusa' (reprinted in *New French Feminisms*, ed. E. Marks and I. de Courtivron) as they explore Offred interior monologues and the importance of body language within Gilead's publicly enforced female silence. Following Cixous, critics like Thompson, Howells, Karen Stein (*Atwood Revisited*), and Michael Greene in his essay 'Body/Language in *The Handmaid's Tale*: Reading Notes' *(Lire Margaret Atwood: The Handmaid's Tale*, ed. M. Dvorak) comment on Offred's poetic language. They analyse her creative use of **metaphors** and her lyrical imagery of flowers and the natural processes of growth and fertility, all signalling a traditionally feminine response to experience and creating what has been called 'the seductive erotics of romantic narrative'. Through her interior monologue Offred continually reminds herself, not only of the past but of her individuality in the present, which exceeds Gilead's definition of her as a 'two-legged womb' (p. 146). From her own perspective Offred's body is more like a wilderness or a dark cosmic landscape, the site of her desires and longings for love or for her grief over the loss of all her family.

Perhaps the most distinctive mark of her individuality is her language, with its irrepressible verbal play and its humour. Her ironic awareness of incongruities, her irreverence, and her sharp critical wit all relate to her dissident feminist critical mode in reaction to patriarchal tyranny. The best analysis of Offred's irony and humour is in Thompson's *Scarlet Letters*, where she compares Offred's narrative voice with that of Charles Dickens: 'The humour is widely varied: irony, including humorous reversals and incongruity; clever wordplay; subversive obscenities; comic self-denigration; in-jokes; and satire' (Thompson, p. 73).

Offred's ironic viewpoint may be related to the ironic view of history which Atwood develops in this novel, shifting the focus to the 'Historical Notes' at the end, where Professor Pieixoto's sexist interpretation of Offred's tale tries to discredit it. Feminist critics highlight Offred's role as Gilead's most reliable historian, though the version she tells is 'herstory', criticised by the professor as irrelevant: 'She could have told us much about the working of the Gileadean empire, had she had the instincts of a reporter or a spy' (p. 322). Much research has been done on the historical relation between American Puritanism and contemporary right-wing fundamentalism, as essays by Mark Evans and Priscilla Ollier-Morin indicate (see **Further reading**). Gilead and Professor Pieixoto with their discourses of power may seem to have silenced Offred, but her voice, transcribed from cassette tapes on to the page in the form of printed words is there at the centre of this novel like a time bomb, ready to deliver its message of defiance and hope to readers at the beginning of the twenty-first century.

> **CONTEXT**
>
> The Victorian novelist Charles Dickens is noted for his skill in mixing the tragic and the grotesquely comic, in novels like *David Copperfield* and *Great Expectations*.

PART FIVE

BACKGROUND

MARGARET ATWOOD

Margaret Atwood would like to clear a few things up from the start. She is not a murderer (this in spite of writing as a murderer in *Alias Grace*). She was not bullied to within an inch of her existence by her childhood best friend (unlike the narrator of *Cat's Eye*). She is not a femme fatale about to steal your man (*The Robber Bride*), she does not have an eating disorder (*The Edible Woman*), and she is not a woman whose lover committed suicide (*Life Before Man*), or a woman searching for her lost father (*Surfacing*). People often think she lives the lives of the characters in her books, she says. But they are not her.

This extract from an interview in the *Guardian* (16 September, 2000) illustrates the wide range of Atwood's fiction, while it also insists on the separation between the writer's life and her novels.

Margaret Atwood is Canada's most famous novelist. She is also the best known feminist novelist writing in English today, and her reputation is world wide. Margaret Atwood is now in her early sixties. Born in Ottawa in 1939, she spent her early childhood moving around rural Ontario and Quebec with her family, as her father was a field entomologist. In 1946 he became a university professor in Toronto, and the family settled there, where Atwood went to high school and to university.

In 1961, the year that she graduated, she had her first book published, a collection of poems entitled *Double Persephone*. Atwood's first experience of the United States of America was in 1961 when she went as a graduate student to Harvard University, where she studied American literature, learned a great deal about seventeenth-century Puritan New England, and realised how little the Americans knew about Canada.

CHECK THE BOOK

For detailed accounts of Atwood's life, see Nathalie Cooke, *Margaret Atwood: A Biography*, 1998, and Rosemary Sullivan, *The Red Shoes: Margaret Atwood Starting Out*, 1998.

HER OTHER WORKS

In 1965 she won Canada's major literary prize, the Governor-General's Award, for her collection of poems *The Circle Game*, and in 1969 her first novel *The Edible Woman* was published. She was extremely productive in the 1970s, publishing three novels – *Surfacing* (1972), *Lady Oracle* (1976), *Life Before Man* (1977); five books of poetry – *The Journals of Susanna Moodie* (1970), *Procedures for Underground* (1970), *Power Politics* (1971), *You Are Happy* (1974) and *Two-Headed Poems* (1978); a book of short stories – *Dancing Girls* (1979); a major work of literary criticism – *Survival: A Thematic Guide to Canadian Literature* (1972); and a children's book – *Up in the Tree* (1978).

As her literary reputation grew, Atwood began travelling extensively to give readings and lectures; she also won many literary prizes. She has continued to travel internationally and to win literary prizes ever since. Her output as poet, novelist and critic has been prodigious: *True Stories* (poetry) and *Bodily Harm* (novel) (1981); *Second Words: Selected Critical Prose* (1982); *Murder in the Dark* (prose poems) and *Bluebeard's Egg* (short stories) (1983); *Interlunar* (poems) (1984); *The Handmaid's Tale* (novel) (1985); *Selected Poems II* (1986); *The Can Lit Food Book* (1987); *Cat's Eye* (novel) (1988); *Margaret Atwood: Conversations* (1990); *Wilderness Tips* (short stories) (1991); *Good Bones* (short fictions) (1992); *The Robber Bride* (novel) (1993); *Morning in the Burned House* (poetry), and *Strange Things: The Malevolent North in Canadian Literature* (criticism) (1995); *Alias Grace* (novel) (1996); The *Blind Assassin* (novel) (2000); and *Negotiating with the Dead: A Writer on Writing* (autobiography and criticism) (2002).

She has also edited *The Oxford Book of Canadian Verse in English* (1982) and co-edited *The Oxford Book of Short Stories in English* (1986) and *The New Oxford Book of Canadian Short Stories in English* (1995). Clearly, Margaret Atwood is dazzlingly proficient in both poetry and prose.

In her novels she has experimented with a range of narrative **genres** from Gothic romances and fairytales to spy thrillers, science fiction utopias and **fictive autobiographies.** *The Handmaid's Tale*

CONTEXT

Gothic novels tend to deal with cruel passions or supernatural terrors and have a gloomy, obsessive, violent and spine-chilling atmosphere.

combines elements from all these, for if one of the distinctive features of her fiction is its experimentalism, another is its thematic continuities. Margaret Atwood has always believed that art has a social function. As she wrote in 1982:

> If writing novels – and reading them – have any redeeming social value, it's probably that they force you to imagine what it's like to be somebody else. Which increasingly is something we all need to know. ('Writing the Male Character', in *Second Words*)

Her novels are eye-witness (I-witness) accounts which focus on contemporary political issues: 'And what do we mean by "political"? What we mean is how people relate to a power structure and vice versa' (*Conversations*). This wide definition of 'politics' accommodates all Atwood's enduring concerns, which we see displayed in the **dystopian** fiction of *The Handmaid's Tale*: her feminism and her scrutiny of male-female relationships, her ecological interests, her nationalist concern with relations between Canada and the United States, and her wider concerns with basic human rights under various forms of state oppression.

In her new novel *Oryx and Crake* (2003) Atwood returns to the genre of science fiction, with an emphasis on environmental disaster and the dangers of genetic engineering rather than gender oppression.

HISTORICAL AND POLITICAL CONTEXT

QUESTION
In interpreting this novel, what matters more: a focus on character, or a focus on politics?

It is to be noted that Gilead has a specifically American location, and Atwood's clippings file for the novel contains a great deal of material on the American New Right in the early 1980s, with its warnings about the 'Birth Dearth', its anti-feminism, its anti-homosexuality, its racism and its strong religious underpinnings in the Bible Belt.

As a coalition of conservative interests which sought to influence government legislation on family issues and public morals, the New Right harked back to America's Puritan inheritance, and was politically powerful under President Reagan and the first President Bush though far less so under President Clinton.

It is an interesting feature of utopias and dystopias that they are always responses to conditions which are causing anxiety at the time of writing, and it is that assault on liberal social policies which is **satirised** in Gilead as representing an extreme version of such ideology in practice. It was in the early 1980s that the religious right wing fundamentalist groups suddenly became a political force in America, with their strong backing for President Reagan and the Republican party.

Much of the strength of the extreme right in this period lay in its women activists like Phyllis Schaffly (another possible model for the Commander's Wife) who travelled round the country making speeches and mobilising women to support right-wing policies on gender and family issues. Thanks largely to lobbying from the Christian right, the Equal Rights Amendment was not ratified in 1982 as envisaged by feminist groups and liberals. Perhaps by a curious coincidence in 1983 a collection of essays on New Right ideology of the family, abortion, pornography, and homosexuality, *The New Right at Harvard*, edited by Howard Phillips, was published. (Photocopies of sections of Phillips's book are collected in the Atwood Papers.) This locational specificity is another reason perhaps why Atwood might have chosen Harvard university as the 'heartland' of Gilead.

Atwood speculates on the mechanisms by which a fundamentalist revolutionary group might seize power and on the ways in which new technology could be used to wipe out democratic freedoms. In this story of gender oppression, one issue which directly affects Offred is the cancellation of women's credit cards, quite unexpectedly, at an early stage of Gilead's social engineering programme, so destroying at one stroke a large measure of women's economic independence and forcing them back into their homes. This move is resented not only by young women like Offred and Moira, but also by older women like the Commander's Wife, who find themselves disempowered and robbed of a public platform within the new ultra-conservative Puritan state of Gilead which, **ironically**, they had done so much to promote.

Atwood's interest in Puritan New England relates to her own ancestry (especially to her relative Mary Webster who was hanged

CONTEXT

The 1980s' fundamentalist right wing in the States was supported by its own political organisation under Rev. Jerry Falwell with his Moral Majority. This was the period of popular television evangelists like Falwell and Jim and Tammy Faye Bakker (who has been cited as a possible model for the Commander's Wife).

as a witch in 1683) and also to her studies at Harvard under Professor Perry Miller, the great scholar of the Puritan mind (see **Summaries**, on **Prefatory material**). Gilead with its passion for traditional values as a way of legitimating the repressive regime as thoroughly 'American', borrows selectively from the historical model of the Puritan forefathers of America: 'The mindset of Gilead is really close to that of the seventeenth-century Puritans' (*Conversations*, p. 223).

As Atwood has pointed out repeatedly, the Puritans aspired to a utopian society, though the system they evolved was oppressive, theocratic and very patriarchal. She quotes Nathaniel Hawthorne's remark that one of the first things built in Puritan New England was a prison and the second was a gallows to hang dissenters. Atwood sees it as the primal tragedy of American history that the nation is based on a failed aspiration to build utopia in the New World. In her reading of contemporary American literature she sees it haunted by the ghost of that failed inheritance:

> Most twentieth-century American literature is about the gap between the promise and the actuality, between the imagined ideal Golden West or the City upon a Hill, the model for all the world postulated by the Puritans, and the actual squalid materialism, dotty small town, nasty city, or redneck-filled outback. (*Survival*, p. 32)

CHECK THE BOOK

Set in seventeenth-century Puritan New England *The Scarlet Letter* (1850) tells the tale of Hester Prynne who refuses to name the father of her illegitimate child, and is persecuted by her community. Her husband sets out to find the natural father, who is a pusillanimous minister, and he hounds him into confession and madness.

Arguably, another reason for her choice of the United States relates directly to its own history, which always contained a dystopia in the making.

Many of the practices of Gilead, especially its attitudes to women as the inferior sex, hark back to the Puritans and Hawthorne's novel *The Scarlet Letter* is one of the literary texts to which Atwood alludes. Perry Miller's histories provide many of the details which are used in the novel, such as the Puritan preachers' reference to women as 'Handmaids of the Lord', and many of the practices connected with childbirth, like the birthing stool or the gathering of all the women as supported in labour and as witnesses to the birth. However, transposing seventeenth-century behaviour and beliefs into the late twentieth century looks like nothing so much as antiquarianism as well as a grotesque **parody** of American Puritan history and a way of degrading female sexuality as dangerously subhuman.

Gilead's attempts to redefine female identity in reductively biological terms provides the opportunity for a scrutiny of North American feminism in its recent history since the 1960s (see **Themes**, on **Feminism**).

Not only does Atwood **satirise** American society, however, for as the 'Historical Notes' indicate, Gilead's tyrannical practices are based on an international range of models which include not only historical examples but also contemporary political atrocities in Latin America, Iran and the Philippines, and today one might add Iraq and Afghanistan. 'Denay Nunavit' (Deny None of It) seems to be Atwood's message out of the past and into the future, shocking readers out of complacency into a recognition of our shared moral responsibility.

LITERARY CONTEXT

Set in a futuristic USA at the beginning of the twenty-first century, *The Handmaid's Tale* belongs to the science fiction **genre** of **dystopian** fiction. Atwood has traced the lineage of her novel through accounts of her adolescent reading of masculinist dystopias from Jonathan Swift's *Gulliver's Travels* through many twentieth-century novels including Yevgeny Zamyatin's *We* (1920–21), Aldous Huxley's *Brave New World* (1932), George Orwell's *Nineteen Eighty –Four* (1949), and Arthur Koestler's *Darkness at Noon* (1940). She was a great fan of John Wyndham, whose 1955 novel *The Chrysalids,* set in Labrador, bears some interesting similarities to *The Handmaid's Tale* with its themes of nuclear holocaust and ecological disaster, here called the 'Tribulation', and its brutal fundamentalist Puritan society which destroys deformed or mutant babies in the name of 'Purity of the Race'. Like all these, *The Handmaid's Tale* projects a nightmare future as prophecy and warning. As Atwood pointed out in a 1986 interview, '*Nineteen Eighty-Four* was written not as science fiction but as an

 CHECK THE NET
The Greenpeace websites are filled with information on environmental issues and current campaigns to protect the global environment. See **http://www. greenpeace.org.**

extrapolation of life in 1948. So, too, *The Handmaid's Tale* is a slight twist on the society we have now'. (Nathalie Cooke, *Margaret Atwood*, p. 277)

Interestingly, there is a specifically Canadian science fiction context for Atwood's novel. Since the 1960s other Canadian novelists had been writing about the dangers of nuclear accidents and warning against ecological disaster. The best known are Phyllis Gotlieb whose *Sunburst* (1964) was set in the near future in Canada, Wayland Drew's *The Wabeno Feast* (1973) which is another scenario of ecological disaster, Michael Coney's *Winter's Children* (1974), and Hugh MacLennan's post-holocaust novel *Voices in Time* (1980). It is Atwood's originality in combining the themes of national disaster with those of Canadian-American relations and a global history of totalitarian oppression, all told from a feminine narrative perspective, which has made *The Handmaid's Tale* such a popular and disturbingly relevant novel.

This is Atwood's trenchant analysis of political power and its abuses. Indeed it is women who are worst off in Gilead, for they are valued only in terms of their biological usefulness as childbearers in a society where, owing to deadly pollution and sexually transmitted diseases, the birth rate has fallen to a catastrophically low level (see **Utopias and dystopias**).

Characteristically, Atwood uses a combination of genres here, for this is also a woman's **fictive autobiography** and a novel of feminist resistance which includes a critical history of North American 'second wave' feminism and a love story. (Faithful to her motif of doubling, there are two love stories – one with Luke and one with Nick – showing Offred's refusal to give up her old-fashioned belief in 'falling in love'.) Offred's style has much in common with women's traditional oral narratives and female gossip. She adopts a feminine form of counter-discourse to Gilead's **rhetoric** in order to claim her own space: 'There has to be some space, finally, that I claim as mine, even in this time,' (p. 60).

Atwood alludes to many other texts in *The Handmaid's Tale*, such as Nathaniel Hawthorne's story of Puritan New England *The Scarlet Letter* (1850), fairytales like Little Red Riding Hood, and Jonathan Swift's social **satire**, *A Modest Proposal* (1729). As she said,

> One of the most allusion-studded things I've done was *The Handmaid's Tale*, the very title of which is an allusion; to Chaucer and also to the Bible. ('On Allusion', *University of Toronto Quarterly*, 61,3, 1992)

Offred's storytelling is an act of resistance to Gilead, just as her tale itself is an act of resistance to masculinist fiction conventions, including that archetypal patriarchal text, the Old Testament. Within the tradition of feminist revisionist fiction Atwood inscribes a woman's viewpoint while still acknowledging, as the critic Linda Hutcheon reminds us,

> the power of the male textual space within which they [women] cannot avoid to some extent operating. (*The Canadian Postmodern*, p. 110)

CHECK THE BOOK

A Modest Proposal's full title continued: *for Preventing the Children of Poor People in Ireland, from Being a Burden to Their Parents or Country; and for Making Them Beneficial to the Publick.* Swift's proposal in this satirical pamphlet was that poor children should be fattened to be fed to the rich.

World events	Author's life	Other literary works
		1850 Nathaniel Hawthorne, *The Scarlet Letter*
		1915 Charlotte Perkins Gilman, *Herland*
		1921 Yevgeny Zamyatin, *My (We)*
1933-45 7 million Jews exterminated under Nazi regime		**1934** Aldous Huxley, *Brave New World*
1939-45 Second World War	**1939** Margaret Atwood born, Ottawa	
	Early 1940s Lives in Rural Ontario where father is entomologist, and Quebec	
	1946 Settles in Toronto, where father becomes a university professor	
		1949 George Orwell, *Nineteen Eighty-Four*. Simone de Beauvoir, *Le Deuxième Sexe (The Second Sex)*
1954 Acid rain first documented		
		1955 *John Wyndham, The Crystalids*
	1961 Graduates, and publishes first poems. Goes to Harvard to study American literature	
1962 Rachel Carson's *Silent Spring* prophesies devastation of our environment through pesticides and pollution		
		1964 Phyllis Gotlieb, *Sunburst*

World events	Author's life	Other literary works
	1966 Publishes *The Circle Game* (poems)	
1967 Abortion legalised in Britain	**1967** Marries James Polk	
1968 Pope Paul's encyclical *Humanae Vitae*: 'Every conjugal act (has) to be open to the transmission of life'		
China legislates only one child per family	**1969** Publishes *The Edible Woman*	
1970 Sun Myung Moon of the Unification Church performs mass marriage ceremony of 790 couples. 2 million die in Biafran civil war		
1971 Greenpeace founded to protest about nuclear testing in Alaska	**1970-8** Publishes five further books of poetry	**1971** Germaine Greer, *The Female Eunuch*
1972 US Congress endorses Equal Rights Amendment	**1972** Publishes *Survival*, controversial study of Canadian literature; *Surfacing* (novel)	
1973 Abortion legalised in USA	**1973** Divorced; lives with partner Graeme Gibson, novelist	**1973** Wayland Drew, *The Wabeno Feast*
1974 International Federation for Family Life Promotion founded in USA (anti-abortion)		**1974** Ursula Le Guin, *The Dispossessed*
1975 War ends in Vietnam Sterilisation of low-caste men in India		**1975** Joanna Russ, *The Female Man*
1975-9 1 million die in Cambodia under Khmer Rouge	**1976** Daughter Jess born. Publishes *Lady Oracle*	**1976** Marge Piercy, *Woman on the Edge of Time*

World events	Author's life	Other literary works
	1977 Publishes *Dancing Girls*	
1978 First test-tube baby, Louise Brown, born		
1979 Women protest against Islamic fundamentalist strictures: 'Freedom, not the chador'	**1979** Publishes *Life Before Man*	
1980 Ronald Reagan becomes President of the United States. Jerry Falwell, of Evangelical Right, publishes *Listen America!*; Richard Viguerie, *The New Right: We're Ready to Lead.* Republican Party withdraws its support to ERA, preventing its ratification. *Death of a Princess* reveals execution for adultery in Saudi Arabia		**1980** Hugh MacLennan, *Voices in Time*
Early 1980s Romania bans birth control	**1981** Publishes *Bodily Harm*. Begins thinking about writing *The Handmaid's Tale*	
1983 Howard Philips, *The New Right at Harvard*		
	1983–4 Publishes *Murder in the Dark*, *Interlunar* (poems) and *Bluebeard's Egg* (short stories)	**1984** Angela Carter, *Nights at the Circus*
	1985 Publishes *THE HANDMAID'S TALE*	**1985** Jeanette Winterson, *Oranges Are Not the Only Fruit*
1986 World's worst nuclear power accident at Chernobyl		
1988 George Bush becomes President of USA; Canadian Multiculturalism Act	**1988** Publishes *Cat's Eye*	

World events	Author's life	Other literary works
1990 Anti-feminist backlash		
Forty-nine Nobel Prize winning scientists appeal to President Bush to curb greenhouse gas emissions	**1991–2** Publishes *Wilderness Tips* (short stories), *Good Bones* (short fictions)	
1992 Bill Clinton becomes President of USA		
	1993 Publishes *The Robber Bride*	**1995** Pat Barker wins the Booker Prize for *The Ghost Road*
1996 Taliban militia establishes Islamic state in Afganistan	**1996** Publishes *Alias Grace*	
Six people fight over legal parenthood of surrogate mother's baby		
2000 George W. Bush becomes President of USA; refuses to sign Kyoto Protocol on climate, withdraws USA from ICBM Treaty on ballistic weapons	**2000** Publishes The *Blind Assassin* and wins Booker Prize	
2001 Bombing of the Trade Centre Towers in New York by Islamic fundamentalists		**2001** Zadie Smith, *White Teeth*
2002 War in Afganistan; Taliban deposed	**2002** Publishes *Negotiating with the Dead: A Writer on Writing*	**2002** Ian McEwan, *Atonement*
2003 Iraq War where coalition of American and British forces deposed Saddam Hussein's regime	**2003** Publishes *Oryx and Crake*	

BACKGROUND READING

Margaret Atwood, *Second Words: Selected Critical Prose*, Anansi, Toronto, 1982. Reprinted 1996
Contains important Atwood essays on 'Witches' and 'Canadian-American Relations: Surviving the Eighties'

Margaret Atwood, *Good Bones*, Virago, 1993

Margaret Atwood, *Eating Fire: Selected Poetry 1965-1995*, Virago, 1998
This collection contains the Orpheus and Eurydice poems

The Bible
especially The Book of Genesis

Nathalie Cooke, *Margaret Atwood: A Biography*, ECW Press, Toronto, 1998
See Chapter 19 which discusses the writing and reception of *The Handmaid's Tale*

Alexander Cruden, *A Concordance to the Old and New Testaments*, ed. C. S. Carey, Routledge, 1925
Indispensable tool for tracing biblical references. Alternatively check Searchable Web Bible http://www.gospelcom.net/bible

Maggie Humm, ed., *Feminisms: A Reader*, Harvester-Wheatsheaf, 1992
Useful anthology for the history of Anglo-American feminism since the 1960s

Earl G. Ingersoll, ed., Margaret Atwood, *Conversations*, Virago, 1992
Contains valuable Atwood interviews on *The Handmaid's Tale*; well indexed

Naomi Klein, *No Logo*, Flamingo, 2000
A factual book on the dangers of consumerist society

Krishan Kumar, *Utopianism*, Open University, Press, 1991
Comprehensive overview of this science fiction genre

Elaine Marks and Isabelle de Courtivron, eds, *New French Feminisms: An Anthology*, Harvester-Wheatsheaf, 1981
Contains essay by Hélène Cixous, 'The Laugh of the Medusa'

Pam Morris, *Literature and Feminism*, Blackwell, 1993
Accessible introduction to feminist literary theory and criticism

George Orwell, *Nineteen Eighty-Four*, Penguin, any edition
  Important model for Atwood's dystopia

Ruth Robbins, *Literary Feminisms*, Macmillan, 2000
  Useful introduction to women's writing and related theoretical issues

Colin Smith, 'Iranian Prisons,' *Observer* (6 June, 1984), 9
  Contains eye witness account of Iranian prison conditions, comparable with Gilead's scenarios

Rosemary Sullivan, *The Red Shoes: Margaret Atwood Starting Out*, 1998
  This entertaining biography focuses on Atwood's formative years in the 1970s

CRITICAL STUDIES

Marta Dvorak, ed., *Lire Margaret Atwood: The Handmaid's Tale*, Presses Universitaires de Rennes, 1999
  Contains important Atwood lecture, *'The Handmaid's Tale : A Feminist Dystopia?'* and Priscilla Ollier-Morin's essay on American Protestant fundamentalism

Dominick Grace, *'The Handmaid's Tale*: Historical Notes and Documentary Subversion,' *Science Fiction Studies* 25, Part 3 (November 1998), 481–94
  This essay analyses how the 'Historical Notes' as a male historian's reconstruction forces re-evaluation of Offred's tale

Coral Ann Howells, *Margaret Atwood*, Macmillan, 1996
  See Chapter 7 for discussion of *The Handmaid's Tale* as science fiction in the feminine

Linda Hutcheon, *The Canadian Postmodern: A Study of Contemporary English-Canadian Fiction*, Oxford University Press, 1988
  See Chapter 7 which discusses Atwood's fiction as Canadian, feminist and **postmodernist**

B.Johnson, 'Language, Power and Responsibility in *The Handmaid's Tale:* Towards a Discourse of Literary Gossip,' *Canadian Literature* 148 (Spring 1996), 39–55
  This essay highlights the power of gossip as language of a women's subculture in Gilead

David Ketterer, *Canadian Science Fiction and Fantasy*, Indiana University Press, 1992.
  Contains a brief discussion of *The Handmaid's Tale* as a 'contextual dystopia'

J.-M. Lacroix and J. Leclaire, eds., *Margaret Atwood: The Handmaid's Tale / Le Conte de la servante: The Power Game*, Presses de la Sorbonne Nouvelle, 1998
   Essays on survival, psychoanalysis, and Atwood's narrative strategies in this novel; six of the nine essays are in English

J.-M. Lacroix, J. Leclaire and J. Warwick, eds., *The Handmaid's Tale: Roman Protéen*, Université de Rouen, 1999
   See informative interview and Round Table with Atwood on genesis of *The Handmaid's Tale;* six of the seven essays are in English

Colin Nicholson, ed., *Margaret Atwood: Writing and Subjectivity*, Macmillan and St Martin's Press, 1994
   This contains excellent essays by Mark Evans on the Puritan background to *The Handmaid's Tale* and by Sherrill Grace on the genre of fictive autobiography

Reingard M. Nischik, ed., *Margaret Atwood: Works and Impact,* Camden House, 2000
   This important collection contains essays setting *The Handmaid's Tale* in context, by Coral Howells on genre and by Lorna Irvine on recycling culture in Gilead

Karen Stein, 'Margaret Atwood's Modest Proposal: *The Handmaid's Tale*', *Canadian Literature*, 148 (Spring 1996), 57–73
   This essay examines the different genre conventions employed in the narrative

Karen Stein, *Margaret Atwood Revisited*, Twayne, 1999
   This is a critical study and overview of Atwood's works in the Twayne World Authors series

Lee Briscoe Thompson, *Scarlet Letters: Margaret Atwood's The Handmaid's Tale*, Toronto, ECW Press, 1998
   Close study of important aspects of the novel in the Canadian Fiction series, 34

Viner, Katherine, 'Double Bluff,' *Guardian* (16 September, 2000), 18–27
   Interview with Atwood on publication of *The Blind Assassin*

Sharon R. Wilson, *Margaret Atwood's Fairy Tale Sexual Politics*, University of Mississippi Press, ECW Press, 1994.
   This both explores Atwood's use of folk tales, fairy tales and legends to give a cultural context for her female story tellers

Sharon R. Wilson, ed. *Margaret Atwood's Textual Assassinations: Recent Poetry and Fiction*, Ohio State University Press, 2003
> These ten essays cover all genres, paying close attention to postmodern, postcolonial, and deconstructive features of Atwood's writings

Lorraine York, ed., *Various Atwoods: Essays on the later poems, short fiction, and novels*, Anansi, 1995
> See essays by Glenn Willmott comparing novel and film version, and by Nathalie Cooke on Atwood's use of confessional novel genre

It's worth watching the film version of *The Handmaid's Tale*, available on video. Compare and contrast the novel and the film, investigating reasons for their differences.

LITERARY TERMS

analogy a parallel word, thing, or idea, used for comparison

double an *alter ego* who bears an uncanny partial resemblance to the self and reveals aspects of the self which have been repressed; in consequence, this 'double' seems both familiar and alien

dystopia anti-utopia, the opposite of utopia; invented futuristic nightmare world based on current social, political and economic trends and warning against their possible disastrous implications

écriture feminine feminine writing, a term borrowed from French feminist theory about signs of gender in writing; it refers to highly **metaphorical**, often unpunctuated flowing writing which represents female body processes and emotional rhythms

epigraph quotations usually found at the beginning of a book, or chapter of a book

euphemism a pleasanter or politer word or phrase used to conceal something unpleasant

fictive autobiography the life story of someone written by him- or herself, which is an invention of the imagination, and not fact

flashback narrative technique which disrupts time sequence by introducing an event or memory which happened in the past prior to the present action of the novel

genre a type of literature, e.g., historical romance, or detective novel, or science fiction

irony covert sarcasm; saying one thing while meaning another; using words to convey the opposite of their literal meaning; saying something that has one meaning for someone knowledgeable about a situation and another meaning for those who are not; incongruity between what might be expected and what actually happens; ill-timed arrival of an event which had been hoped for

metaphor figure of speech in which a descriptive term, or name or action characteristic of one object is applied to another to suggest a likeness between them, but which does not use 'like' or 'as' in the comparison

narratology the study and theory of the ways a story can be told

palimpsest originally a manuscript on which the writing has been partially erased but is still visible when written over again (and invaluable in historical research). It has come to mean a much amended and revised text

paradox a statement that seems self-contradictory; something which seems absurd or unbelievable, yet which may be true

parody a humorous or ludicrous imitation of a piece of serious writing or speech

postmodern as literary practice refers to contemporary writing which self-consciously draws attention to its own **rhetorical** techniques and narrative artifice, so disrupting conventions of realism, commenting 'metafictively' on writing as process, challenging the borderlines between fact and fictions, and problematising the relation between creative writing and critical commentary

propaganda literature, often polemical, designed to persuade a reader or audience to a given cause

rhetoric grandiloquent or affected speech that is often lacking in sincerity or content

satire literature that explores vice or folly and makes them appear ridiculous; usually morally censorious

selfconscious narrator narrator who reveals to the reader that the story is a fabrication, and who comments within the text on the storytelling process in order to emphasise the gap between fiction and reality

symbol something that by association in thought comes to represent something else; often an object that represents something abstract, such as an idea, quality or condition

thematic motif a recurrent element which is significant in the overall structure of meaning in the text

Coral Ann Howells studied at the Universities of Queensland and London and is Professor of English and Canadian Literature at the University of Reading. She is author of *Margaret Atwood*, Macmillan, 1996, *Alice Munro*, Manchester University Press, 1998, and *Contemporary Canadian Women's Fiction: Refiguring Identities*, Palgrave, 2003.

General editors

Martin Gray, former Head of the Department of English Studies at the University of Stirling, and of Literary Studies at the University of Luton

Professor A. N. Jeffares, Emeritus Professor of English, University of Stirling

Maya Angelou
I Know Why the Caged Bird Sings

Jane Austen
Pride and Prejudice

Alan Ayckbourn
Absent Friends

Elizabeth Barrett Browning
Selected Poems

Robert Bolt
A Man for All Seasons

Harold Brighouse
Hobson's Choice

Charlotte Brontë
Jane Eyre

Emily Brontë
Wuthering Heights

Shelagh Delaney
A Taste of Honey

Charles Dickens
David Copperfield
Great Expectations
Hard Times
Oliver Twist

Roddy Doyle
Paddy Clarke Ha Ha Ha

George Eliot
Silas Marner
The Mill on the Floss

Anne Frank
The Diary of a Young Girl

William Golding
Lord of the Flies

Oliver Goldsmith
She Stoops to Conquer

Willis Hall
The Long and the Short and the Tall

Thomas Hardy
Far from the Madding Crowd
The Mayor of Casterbridge
Tess of the d'Urbervilles
The Withered Arm and other Wessex Tales

L.P. Hartley
The Go-Between

Seamus Heaney
Selected Poems

Susan Hill
I'm the King of the Castle

Barry Hines
A Kestrel for a Knave

Louise Lawrence
Children of the Dust

Harper Lee
To Kill a Mockingbird

Laurie Lee
Cider with Rosie

Arthur Miller
The Crucible
A View from the Bridge

Robert O'Brien
Z for Zachariah

Frank O'Connor
My Oedipus Complex and Other Stories

George Orwell
Animal Farm

J.B. Priestley
An Inspector Calls
When We Are Married

Willy Russell
Educating Rita
Our Day Out

J.D. Salinger
The Catcher in the Rye

William Shakespeare
Henry IV Part I
Henry V
Julius Caesar
Macbeth
The Merchant of Venice
A Midsummer Night's Dream
Much Ado About Nothing
Romeo and Juliet
The Tempest
Twelfth Night

George Bernard Shaw
Pygmalion

Mary Shelley
Frankenstein

R.C. Sherriff
Journey's End

Rukshana Smith
Salt on the snow

John Steinbeck
Of Mice and Men

Robert Louis Stevenson
Dr Jekyll and Mr Hyde

Jonathan Swift
Gulliver's Travels

Robert Swindells
Daz 4 Zoe

Mildred D. Taylor
Roll of Thunder, Hear My Cry

Mark Twain
Huckleberry Finn

James Watson
Talking in Whispers

Edith Wharton
Ethan Frome

William Wordsworth
Selected Poems

A Choice of Poets

Mystery Stories of the Nineteenth Century including The Signalman

Nineteenth Century Short Stories

Poetry of the First World War

Six Women Poets

For the AQA Anthology:

Duffy and Armitage & Pre-1914 Poetry

Heaney and Clarke & Pre-1914 Poetry

Poems from Different Cultures

Margaret Atwood
Cat's Eye
The Handmaid's Tale

Jane Austen
Emma
Mansfield Park
Persuasion
Pride and Prejudice
Sense and Sensibility

Alan Bennett
Talking Heads

William Blake
*Songs of Innocence and of
Experience*

Charlotte Brontë
Jane Eyre
Villette

Emily Brontë
Wuthering Heights

Angela Carter
Nights at the Circus

Geoffrey Chaucer
The Franklin's Prologue and Tale
*The Merchant's Prologue and
Tale*
The Miller's Prologue and Tale
*The Prologue to the Canterbury
Tales*
*The Wife of Bath's Prologue and
Tale*

Samuel Coleridge
Selected Poems

Joseph Conrad
Heart of Darkness

Daniel Defoe
Moll Flanders

Charles Dickens
Bleak House
Great Expectations
Hard Times

Emily Dickinson
Selected Poems

John Donne
Selected Poems

Carol Ann Duffy
Selected Poems

George Eliot
Middlemarch
The Mill on the Floss

T.S. Eliot
Selected Poems
The Waste Land

F. Scott Fitzgerald
The Great Gatsby

E.M. Forster
A Passage to India

Brian Friel
Translations

Thomas Hardy
Jude the Obscure
The Mayor of Casterbridge
The Return of the Native
Selected Poems
Tess of the d'Urbervilles

Seamus Heaney
*Selected Poems from 'Opened
Ground'*

Nathaniel Hawthorne
The Scarlet Letter

Homer
The Iliad
The Odyssey

Aldous Huxley
Brave New World

Kazuo Ishiguro
The Remains of the Day

Ben Jonson
The Alchemist

James Joyce
Dubliners

John Keats
Selected Poems

Philip Larkin
*The Whitsun Weddings and
Selected Poems*

Christopher Marlowe
Doctor Faustus
Edward II

Arthur Miller
Death of a Salesman

John Milton
Paradise Lost Books I & II

Toni Morrison
Beloved

George Orwell
Nineteen Eighty-Four

Sylvia Plath
Selected Poems

Alexander Pope
*Rape of the Lock & Selected
Poems*

William Shakespeare
Antony and Cleopatra
As You Like It
Hamlet
Henry IV Part I
King Lear
Macbeth
Measure for Measure
The Merchant of Venice
A Midsummer Night's Dream
Much Ado About Nothing
Othello
Richard II
Richard III
Romeo and Juliet
The Taming of the Shrew
The Tempest
Twelfth Night
The Winter's Tale

George Bernard Shaw
Saint Joan

Mary Shelley
Frankenstein

Jonathan Swift
*Gulliver's Travels and A Modest
Proposal*

Alfred Tennyson
Selected Poems

Virgil
The Aeneid

Alice Walker
The Color Purple

Oscar Wilde
*The Importance of Being
Earnest*

Tennessee Williams
A Streetcar Named Desire
The Glass Menagerie

Jeanette Winterson
Oranges Are Not the Only Fruit

John Webster
The Duchess of Malfi

Virginia Woolf
To the Lighthouse

William Wordsworth
The Prelude and Selected Poems

W.B. Yeats
Selected Poems

Metaphysical Poets

The ultimate web site for the ultimate literature guides

At York Notes we believe in helping you achieve exam success. Log on to **www.yorknotes.com** and see how we have made revision even easier, with over 300 titles available to download twenty-four hours a day. The downloads have lots of additional features such as pop-up boxes providing instant glossary definitions, user-friendly links to every part of the guide, and scanned illustrations offering visual appeal. All you need to do is log on to **www.yorknotes.com** and download the books you need to help you achieve exam success.

Key Features:

Details on how York Notes can help you

Menu Bar to help you find your way around the site

Details on how to download York Notes

Quick Search facility to help you find the titles you need

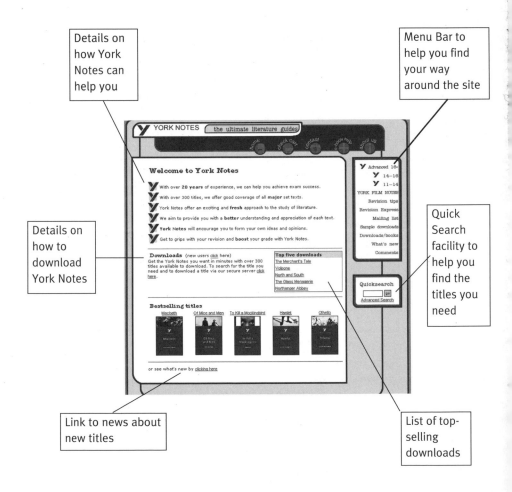

Link to news about new titles

List of top-selling downloads